ESCHATOLOGY

GUIDES TO THEOLOGY

Sponsored by the Christian Theological Research Fellowship

EDITORS

Alan G. Padgett • *Luther Seminary*

David A. S. Fergusson • *University of Edinburgh*

Iain R. Torrance • *University of Aberdeen*

Danielle Nussberger • *Marquette University*

Systematic theology is undergoing a renaissance. Conferences, journal articles, and books give witness to the growing vitality of the discipline. The Christian Theological Research Fellowship is one sign of this development. To stimulate further study and inquiry into Christian doctrine, we are sponsoring, with the William B. Eerdmans Publishing Company, a series of readable and brief introductions to theology.

This series of Guides to Theology is written primarily with students in mind. We also hope that pastors, church leaders, and theologians will find them to be useful introductions to the field. Our aim is to provide a brief introduction to the chosen field, followed by an annotated bibliography of important works, which should serve as an entrée to the topic. The books in this series will be of two kinds. Some volumes, like *The Trinity*, will cover standard theological *loci*. Other volumes will be devoted to various modern approaches to Christian theology as a whole, such as feminist theology or liberation theology. The authors and editors alike pray that these works will help further the faithful study of Christian theology in our time.

ESCHATOLOGY

John C. McDowell and Scott A. Kirkland

WILLIAM B. EERDMANS PUBLISHING COMPANY
GRAND RAPIDS, MICHIGAN

Wm. B. Eerdmans Publishing Co.
4035 Park East Court SE, Grand Rapids, Michigan 49546
www.eerdmans.com

27 26 25 24 23 22 21 20 19 18   1 2 3 4 5 6 7 8 9 10

ISBN 978-0-8028-6458-1

Library of Congress Cataloging-in-Publication Data

Names: McDowell, John C., author.
Title: Eschatology / John C. McDowell and Scott A. Kirkland.
Description: Grand Rapids : Eerdmans Publishing Co., 2018. | Series: Guides
    to theology | Includes bibliographical references and index.
Identifiers: LCCN 2018018270 | ISBN 9780802864581 (pbk. : alk. paper)
Subjects: LCSH: Eschatology.
Classification: LCC BT821.3 .M44 2018 | DDC 236—dc23
    LC record available at https://lccn.loc.gov/2018018270

For the Reverend John Carrick, the inspiration behind the book

Contents

Acknowledgments

This book has been a considerable number of years in the making, or rather on the back of John's research shelf. It was in the mid-2000s that he was approached to contribute to the series, coming off the back of an intense eschatological interest that had generated a doctoral thesis and a number of publications on the account of hope provided by Karl Barth and George Steiner. A move to Australia resulted in this project being deferred continually. The more recent relocating to Melbourne has reignited possibilities for theological reflection, and the substantial addition of Dr. Scott Kirkland to the writing team has resulted in its completion. John would therefore very much like to thank the series editors, Profs. Alan Padgett and David Fergusson, as well as the publisher, William B. Eerdmans, for their very patient hope.

John would like to thank his father-in-law, Rev. John Carrick, for encouraging the early research interest in eschatological matters; Prof. Nicholas Lash for eruditely guiding the doctoral research; and Dr. Scott Kirkland for his invaluable aid in getting the project kicked off again and brought to a timely conclusion. John would finally like to give special thanks to his wife, Sandra, and children Archie, Jonathan, Joseph, Meg, and Robert. They have had to endure yet another work-life imbalanced year. Their hope is that the new year may bring something different.

Scott would like to thank Prof. John C. McDowell for bringing him onto this project, which has proven to be yet another opportunity to learn from John's expertise as well as an occasion to enjoy thinking together. Scott would also like to thank his loving wife, Lisa, who continues to support his work beyond merit, and his mother, Joanna, who taught him to hope in the face of inexplicable loss.

JOHN C. MCDOWELL
Director of Research
University of Divinity
Melbourne

SCOTT A. KIRKLAND
Trinity College
University of Divinity
Melbourne

Introduction

This book takes a slightly different pathway to that charted by some of the earlier volumes in this Guides to Theology series by clustering sets of questions around some dominant themes.

The New Testament writers, like the writers of the Old Testament or Hebrew Scriptures, develop several images through which they express various aspects of the eschatological implications of witness to Jesus as the Christ. These are particularly important: the kingdom of God, eternal life, resurrection and immortality, Jesus Christ as Second Adam, the coming again of Christ, and the new creation, to name only a few.

Yet even here the devil is in the details. For example, while numerous texts are considered in each of the chapters in the present volume under a dominant interpretative theme, nonetheless the work that these texts often do in illuminating the theme can be quite different because of their markedly different contexts. A real danger of appealing to the biblical materials and imagery is that this approach can, unless handled very carefully, give the impression that what is being described is precisely "what the Bible says." This, however, does not pay sufficient attention to the way readers' perspectives can be imposed on the material and the variety of ways in which it is actually read. William Blake offers an appropriate caution here: "Both read the Bible day and night / But thou read'st black where I read white."[1] Not only can different texts be selected and offered in different social and historical

1. William Blake, *The Everlasting Gospel* (1808), quoted in Christopher Rowland, "Scripture: New Testament," in *The Blackwell Companion to Political Theology*, ed. Peter Scott and William T. Cavanaugh (Malden: Blackwell, 2004), 21.

contexts, but even the way those texts are understood can be markedly differ-ent under those different conditions. As Blake suggests, one might very well wonder how it is that two different readers are able to read the same texts in such dissimilar fashions. For this reason, the "back to the Bible" strategies that react negatively to talk of tradition or theology's history, for example, fail to pay attention to their own interpretative contexts and to the ways in which talk of the "biblical message" or of "biblical theology" is colored pre-cisely by those contextual lenses. John Calvin famously used the image of the Scriptures as a pair of spectacles in his *Institutes*. But church fathers such as Irenaeus of Lyons or Augustine of Hippo, among many others, recognized that even reading the Scriptures appropriately involves a life-long process of learning how to read the Scriptures. Calvin's image, then, might be extended to the notion of the Christian traditions (or historical perspectives) as ways of training readers in how to read the Scriptures themselves.[2]

The volume is structured thematically in four main chapters, partly following Karl Rahner's three categories of "apocalyptic," "existential," and "Christologically anthropological" in his paper entitled "Hermeneutics of Eschatological Assertions," but adding a political outlook to those. It then finishes off with an annotated bibliography. Readers should notice that there is no independent chapter on "the last things." The book offers a series of lenses on understanding eschatological statements, or what the content of Christian hope is, and therefore the images of what are often called "the last things" are suffused through these. Also, there is little discussion of the means of or conditions for hope, such as the church as the provisional assem-bly of God's people, the sacraments of baptism and the Eucharist as means of grace, and the Christian life as witness to the shape of the consummated life or the new life to come.

The thematic arrangement of the chapters will take something of a "history of ideas" approach. This makes it easier to locate the perspectives within their historical contexts, and also to observe the way these perspec-tives themselves changed over time.

Chapter 1 will focus on what is commonly called apocalyptic. After tracing this through several moments in the biblical witness, the chapter will move on to cover various apocalyptic movements in the medieval and Reformation periods in the West, finishing with a brief discussion of various

2. We will need to leave this claim for now, but can refer the reader to Augustine, *De Doctrina Christiana* (On Christian Teaching), ed. and trans. R. P. H. Green (Oxford: Claren-don, 1995).

apocalyptic motifs in more recent thought. The eschatological imagery that is often prominent within this set of perspectives is that of the last judgment and heaven and hell.

Chapter 2 reflects on what was once known as an existential approach to eschatological matters. Anthropological interests can be discerned in the second- and third-century Alexandrian tradition, and here Clement of Alexandria serves as an example. This approach takes a markedly different form with the European Enlightenments. Finally, Rudolf Bultmann serves as a twentieth-century guide to an existential approach to eschatological matters of hope.

Chapter 3 focuses on the political dimension of Christian eschatologies, some of which have already been mentioned in the first chapter. Here a reading of the politics of the Gospel theme of the kingdom of God is followed by a consideration of Augustine's *City of God* and the developments of a millenarian perspective among the British and American Puritans in the seventeenth century. The chapter then proceeds to discuss the late-twentieth-century "theology of hope" of Jürgen Moltmann and of the distinctive work of a variety of liberation theologies. The eschatological motif that is prominent here is that of the millennium.

Chapter 4 considers the development of a christological reading of eschatological claims and the hope they generate and ground. The Fourth Gospel is of particular significance here, and from there the chapter goes on to discuss the eschatological approaches of Irenaeus, Athanasius, and Karl Barth. The eschatological themes that often feature substantially in this set of perspectives are those of the *parousia* of God in Christ and the universality of God's saving presence.

A conclusion offers a number of observations on matters concerning Christian hope today.

The final section of the book provides an annotated bibliography, which not only offers particular help in following up any of the themes or writers covered by the first four chapters, out of a truly massive corpus of writing, but also provides a description of some important works that could not be easily fitted into the chapters themselves.

1. Apocalyptic

Apocalyptic, the first of Karl Rahner's approaches, is notoriously difficult to define. Popularly, when we think of apocalyptic we might think of the current resurgence of zombie films and dystopian science fiction such as *World War Z* or *Children of Men*. We may think back to that most evocative use of apocalyptic images in times of war in Francis Ford Coppola's *Apocalypse Now*. Or, indeed, we may think of the predictions of Hal Lindsey's *The Late Great Planet Earth* and Tim LaHaye's *Left Behind* novels. All of these texts draw in one way or another upon a set of ancient traditions that proclaim extravagant visions, dreams, predictions, and political critique.

Apocalypsis means "unveiling," peeling back appearances and seeing things as they really are. The fabulous and strange ancient texts that claim to do this, however, have a complicated history of interpretation and use. Different philosophical, theological, and historical pressures send readers of these texts in differing directions. Apocalyptic images are flexible, and they have been the instrument of church reform, political critique, quietism, speculation regarding the future, and nationalism. In particular, two different kinds of approaches to the book of Revelation bear themselves out throughout history. The first, decoding, is concerned with mapping history onto apocalyptic timelines. The second, actualizing, is interested in the constant reappropriation of apocalyptic images in differing circumstances. Each of these types will emerge under varying contextual circumstances.

New Testament Apocalyptic

Gospels

While apocalyptic is a specific genre in Hebrew literature, it is valuable to draw our attention briefly to the similarities in patterns and expectations surrounding Jesus in the Gospel narratives. Of particular interest are the immediate social and political expectations surrounding Christ's coming. This is evident in the Gospel of Luke, who is deliberate in his marking of historical events. He opens his text by noting that these events are taking place under Herod (Luke 1:5), a man despised by many for cozying up to the oppressive Romans. This is "more than a vague chronological marker, but locates the events in a particular period of political tension."[1] The prophecy of Gabriel (Luke 1:32) that Jesus will be the new king in the line of David positions the events of the Gospels in the midst of real social-historical tensions as Herod's legitimacy is questioned by this child. In Luke's version of the Magnificat, Mary praises God's reversals of the hierarchical social order:

> He has shown strength with his arm;
> > he has scattered the proud in the thoughts of their hearts.
> He has brought down the powerful from their thrones,
> > and lifted up the lowly;
> he has filled the hungry with good things,
> > and sent the rich away empty. (Luke 1:51–53)

The Magnificat draws an immediate link between Jesus who is to come and a radically new social order. This is amplified by the way in which it echoes Hannah's song (1 Sam. 2), which anticipates the coming of the judge, Samuel. There is a further immediate sign of hope in Elizabeth, who is pregnant with John the Baptist after being barren her whole life (Luke 1:7). Right at the start of Luke's Gospel it becomes evident that God is ushering in abrupt and radical change: lifting the lowly, filling the hungry, etc.

As the Gospel continues, tensions grow between the established political power and the alternate order of John the Baptist and Jesus, and apocalyptic imagery follows. John the Baptist proclaims to the crowds, "Even now the ax is lying at the root of the trees; every tree therefore that does not bear good fruit is cut down and thrown into the fire" (Luke 3:9). As Jesus is baptized

---

1. Joel B. Green, *The Gospel of Luke* (Grand Rapids: Eerdmans, 1997), 58.

in the Jordan and proclaimed as God's Son, the heavens are torn open and a dove descends. "This scene is set in the world of apocalyptic with its emphasis on the unveiling of divine mystery. The opening of heaven is familiar from apocalyptic literature, as is the heavenly voice."[2] The significance of this is that we are given a glimpse into the invisible order that is God's true ordering of things. Throughout the Gospel, this tension remains between the invisible and real power of Jesus and the visible and false power of the authorities. This is the heart of apocalyptic tension.

The most explicit apocalyptic scene in the Gospel narratives is that which both Luke and Matthew adapt from Mark 13, the Olivet discourse. Here Jesus foretells the destruction of the temple (Mark 13:1-2), which later occurred historically when the Romans tore it down in 70 CE. In this scene Jesus offers a series of signs, culminating in the coming of the Son of Man in the clouds, an image from Daniel 7:13-14. Many interpret the signs as entirely bound up with the destruction of the temple. Others see the text as a prophecy of future historical events.[3] It is important to note Mark's positioning of the discourse between the end of Jesus's public ministry (Mark 1-12) and the beginning of the events leading to his condemnation, death, and resurrection (Mark 14-16). This is significant because of the recurring reference to the destruction of the temple in the context of Jesus's trial, which "points to the relationship which exists between the judgement upon Jerusalem implied by the discourse and the death of Jesus."[4] Speaking to a specific community facing pressure from Roman authorities, to whom prophecies of a far-off future were of little value, "Mark cautions his readers that the community is to find its authentic eschatological dimension not in apocalyptic fervor but in obedience to Jesus' call to cross-bearing and evangelism in the confidence that this is the will of God which must be fulfilled before the parousia."[5]

Revelation

The book of Revelation represents the most sustained and explicit version of Jewish apocalyptic in the New Testament. It is from this book that such

2. Green, *The Gospel of Luke*, 185. Examples include Ezek. 1:1, 25, 28-21; Rev. 4:1; 10:4; 19:11.

3. See G. R. Beasley-Murray, *Jesus and the Last Days: An Interpretation of the Olivet Discourse* (Vancouver: Regent College Publishing, 2005); L. Gaston, *No Stone on Another: Studies in the Significance of the Fall of Jerusalem in the Synoptic Gospels* (Leiden: Brill, 1970).

4. William L. Lane, *The Gospel of Mark* (Grand Rapids: Eerdmans, 1974), 444.

5. Lane, *The Gospel of Mark*, 447.

ideas as "Armageddon," the "tribulation," and the "millennium" come. It has therefore been at the center of much interpretative debate, particularly since the development of dispensationalism (discussed later in this chapter). Interpretations of Revelation range from the historical reconstructions of Hal Lindsey, which turn John's prophecy into a roadmap of the end of the world, to those who see the text as purely a piece of politically seditious and coded literature wholly bound up with the concerns of the late first century.[6]

Revelation can be reasonably comfortably positioned in the family of Jewish apocalyptic literature. It shares much of its "angelology and preoccupation with the hidden" with texts such as 1 Enoch, Daniel, and 4 Ezra.[7] However, there are distinguishing features owing to the text's preoccupation with the Christian narratives and its distinctive historical location. This can be seen in the way Daniel is habilitated by Revelation. While the two texts are remarkably similar at points in their use of the image of the Son of Man (Dan. 7:13–14; Rev. 1:13) and the spectacular visions of beasts (Dan. 4:1–27; 7:1–8; Rev. 13), there are also marked differences. The author of Daniel remains unknown throughout the text, whereas John identifies himself (Rev. 1:1); the visions in Daniel are followed by interpretations, whereas this device is used only infrequently in Revelation; Daniel often sheds positive light upon the empire through the obedience of rulers, whereas Revelation is much more skeptical of imperial authority.[8] There is a much sharper line between Babylon (Rome) and God in Revelation than in Daniel, where the figure of Daniel himself serves in the courts of the rulers and garners their favor. This reflects differing political circumstances, particularly given Rome's destruction of the Jerusalem temple and the growing numbers of gentile Christian converts, alongside the expectation among early Christian communities that Jesus would return imminently.

Judith Kovacs and Christopher Rowland helpfully distinguish between "decoding" and "actualization" as modes of interpreting Revelation. Decoding "involves presenting the meaning of the text in another, less allusive form, showing what the text *really* means, with great attention to the details." Actualizing "means reading the Apocalypse in relation to new circumstances, seeking to convey the spirit of the text rather than being concerned

6. Judith Kovacs and Christopher Rowland, *Revelation* (Oxford: Wiley Blackwell, 2004), 3. The relation of all first-century apocalyptic to the fall of the Jerusalem temple is always significant.

7. Kovacs and Rowland, *Revelation*, 3.

8. Richard Bauckham, *The Theology of the Book of Revelation* (Cambridge: Cambridge University Press, 1993), 89–90.

with the plethora of detail. Such interpretation tends to regard the text as multivalent, having more than one meaning."[9]

This broad distinction helps us to think about both the way we interpret the significance of the images used in relation to future or past events and, alternatively, their symbolic significance. For example, if we are intent upon decoding the text, we are going to be interested in locating precise historical events that line up with the events in the text. For example, Hal Lindsey "sees in Rev. 9 a description of an all-out attack of ballistic missiles on the cities of the world."[10] This means that there are both events in Revelation that have been fulfilled in some past circumstance and events that remain to be fulfilled in some person or circumstance. If, on the other hand, we adopt an actualizing interpretation, this could take one of two forms. First, we might be inclined to reappropriate the imagery of Revelation to fit our own circumstances. So, for instance, the figure of the beast (Rev. 13) might not be one monstrous figure to appear at the culmination of a long history of tribulation (as we shall see in dispensationalism), but rather a type that can recur again and again. Second, "there is the appropriation by visionaries, where the words of the Apocalypse either offer the opportunity to 'see again' things similar to what had appeared to John or prompt new visions related to it."[11] Neither of these forms of actualization is interested in treating Revelation as a timeline of world history; rather, they see it as a resource for rethinking the position of the believer again and again relative to political and cosmic location. This later actualizing type of interpretation is the most dominant in the history of interpretation.

Both in the Gospels' use of apocalyptic and in Revelation we can see immediate political and social realities in reference to which the texts are to be read. Beginning in the late Middle Ages and in the Reformation, a form of futurist apocalyptic emerged that began to be more concerned with timelines for world history and divine action. This, in turn, affected the ways in which New Testament apocalyptic was read.

---

9. Kovacs and Rowland, *Revelation*, 8.

10. Kovacs and Rowland, *Revelation*, 8, referencing Hal Lindsey, *Late Great Planet Earth* (London: Lakeland, 1970), 87–102.

11. Kovacs and Rowland, *Revelation*, 8.

Medieval Apocalypticism

The fount of western medieval theology, Augustine of Hippo, was decidedly uninterested in speculation concerning the end of the world, and he remained ambivalent to speculation regarding the millennium, as did many of the later fathers. Augustine's sensibility carried a great deal of weight in the early Middle Ages. However, come the tenth century, the apocalyptic heat began to be turned up again with the coming "terror of the year 1000." As the end of the millennium approached, speculation regarding the return of Christ emerged with renewed vigor. The obvious reason for this was that the year 1000 marked a millennium since Christ's birth.

Despite the ambivalence of the church fathers regarding the end of the world, there was a continued fascination with apocalyptic imagery throughout the early Middle Ages, evidenced in ongoing images and legends such as the legend of the Last Roman Emperor. After the destabilization of the western empire through various raids on Rome and the emergence of Islam as a threat to Roman provinces in the eighth and ninth centuries, a myth arose in the Eastern Empire that there would come a time when a final emperor would emerge who would destroy all opponents of Christianity, restore Christian preeminence and peace, and finally step down from power, allowing for the time of the Antichrist. This mixture of Roman and Christian mythology was characteristic of the period. This illustrates the fact that the second millennium of Christian thought was an environment radically different from that faced by the first Christian apocalypse, Revelation. As a consequence of the Christianization of imperial power, one of the big questions facing the church was how to appropriately reform or renew itself so as to avoid manifest corruption here and now. Often we think of the European Middle Ages as a single, continuous period of Christian hegemony. However, this is to do a disservice to the multiplicity of movements for change that emerged in the period. One such tactic for change was the deployment of apocalyptic imagery. As we shall see, in this sense the Protestant reformers were very much in continuity with something internal to the Christian tradition, the ability to develop modes of self-criticism.

Gregorian Reform

One such early catalyst for reform occurred in the eleventh century, the Great Reform associated with Pope Gregory VII, or Hildebrand (1073–1085). In spite of the differences between the book of Revelation and medieval apocalyptic, one element is particularly pertinent as far as the Great Reform is concerned: Gregory seems to have been motivated by the possibility of an imminent return of Christ. He wrote, "For the nearer the day of the Antichrist approaches, the harder he fights to crush out the Christian faith."[12]

Gregory set about a deliberate process of institutional reform, explicitly in anticipation of the last days. The nearer the day of the Antichrist, the more intense the pressures would become. Gregory "and the circle of reformers around him began as monastic reformers, and there was a strong monastic flavour to their attempts to realise the true 'order' (*ordo*) of Christian freedom in the world."[13] Throughout the Middle Ages monastic movements were crucial to the church's ability to maintain a form of self-criticism and continual reform. Gregory, having strong monastic influence, felt the need to reform. What is important to note here is how time in the present was understood to be pressured by the imminence of the end, and alongside this understanding a form of awareness of historical location was beginning to emerge.

This form of historical awareness and use of apocalyptic imagery to dramatize current events can be seen in Rupert of Deutz (1070–1129), who wrote a poem entitled "The Calamities of the Church of Liège." In this poem he applies images from Revelation to speak of the conduct of the diocese of Liège. For example, deploying an image from Revelation 13:1a ("And I saw a beast rising out of the sea, having ten horns and seven heads"), Rupert writes, "Now the ancient enemy arises from the sea, / and rules as victor over the seven hills."[14] Throughout his text Rupert is concerned with thinking through the conflict between the emperor, Henry IV, and Pope Gregory VII—Rupert's hero. This dramatization of current historical events in apocalyptic imagery offers a commentary on Revelation that breaks "with the seven-hundred-year Latin tradition of essentially moral exegesis of the text by suggesting that the Apocalypse might contain prophecies that could also illuminate present and imminent events."[15]

Gregorian reform and its apocalyptic associations continued on throughout the twelfth century in a number of different figures. The century was shaped by a concern, particularly among monastic figures such as Joachim of

12. Pope Gregory VII, *Collected Letters* 9.46, quoted in Bernard McGinn, "Apocalypticism and Church Reform 1100–1500," in *Encyclopedia of Apocalypticism*, vol. 2: *Apocalypticism in Western History and Culture*, ed. Bernard McGinn (London: Bloomsbury, 2000), 76.

13. McGinn, "Apocalypticism and Church Reform 1100–1500," 77.

14. Translation in Bernard McGinn, *Visions of the End: Apocalyptic Traditions in the Middle Ages* (New York: Columbia University Press, 1979), 97.

15. McGinn, "Apocalypticism and Church Reform 1100–1500," 82.

Fiore, about the significance of history and the interpretation of events, given the assumption that God governs history.[16] This concern arose in part because of the way monks were intellectually situated. "If we look for the milieu that situated these minds, we would find it not in the schools but in those places, spiritual after their own fashion, where history was being made more visibly, at least in those times: in the entourages of princes and emperors."[17] For it was in the imperial courts that monks served both as historians and as spiritual advisors to those in power. They were intellectually and spiritually formed by their tasks as chroniclers and advisors. Hence historical patterns and the nature of history itself became of interest to them. Further, in contrast to the theology of the schoolmen, who were concerned largely with more formal philosophical problems, these monastic thinkers started to think of God and nature in more historicized terms, so that "the works and deeds of humanity, under the providence of God—the God of the Bible and not of Nature, God as Redeemer and not as the One—comprised a 'universe' other than the physical one: the human universe of sacred history."[18]

Joachim of Fiore (1135–1202)

Joachim of Fiore is illustrative of this further radicalization of apocalyptic imagery and the beginnings of its historicization, which continues through to contemporary forms of Protestant dispensationalism. Joachim was a monk of the Cistercian order and founded a monastic order of San Giovanni at Fiore (or Flora) in Calabria, in modern southern Italy. Deeply concerned about the morally lax conditions within the church, he was encouraged in his work by Pope Lucius III. He wrote down his apocalyptic interpretations of the Scriptures particularly in *Exposition on the Apocalypse*. "In contrast with 'the perfection of the primitive church,' whose prelates had 'begun to cross over from vices to virtues,' there stood 'the church of the present time,' to which it was appropriate to apply the words of the prophet about Jerusalem: 'How has the faithful city become a harlot!'"[19]

16. M.-D. Chenu, *Nature, Man, and Society in the Twelfth Century* (Chicago: University of Chicago Press, 1968).

17. Chenu, *Nature, Man, and Society*, 164.

18. Chenu, *Nature, Man, and Society*, 163.

19. Jaroslav Pelikan, *The Christian Tradition: A History of the Development of Doctrine*, vol. 3: *The Growth of Medieval Theology (600–1300)* (Chicago: University of Chicago Press, 1978), 301.

Joachim's millenarianism offered a threefold pattern for understanding salvation history, with each period corresponding to a divine person of the Triune God: the epoch of the Father (corresponding to the period of the Old Testament, and characterized by obedience to the Law of God); the epoch of the Son (the New Testament period of Christ and the church, characterized by the coming of grace); and the epoch of the Spirit (a reformist period yet to come, characterized by universal love). Each age, he held, was of forty-two generations (a generation being thirty years), and he expected the age of the Spirit to begin in 1260. In his *Harmony of the New and the Old Testaments*, Joachim declared, "It is our intention . . . to comprehend the end of the temporal realm, which is properly called Babylon, and to disclose in the clearest possible words that which is near, the birth of the church, which will take place at the same time."[20]

Since he seems to have equated the age of the Spirit with the millennium after the defeat of the Antichrist, it would follow that the Antichrist was already born and would shortly raise his head. According to Joachim, the "Antichrist is already born in the city of Rome, and will be elevated to the Apostolic See."[21] While it is unlikely that Joachim equated the office of the papacy itself, and therefore every pope, with the Antichrist, precisely this association was indeed made by others.

> Joachim can hardly have meant to identify the Pope with Antichrist, since he remained on good terms with the Popes of his day. Probably he envisaged some kind of usurpation of the Papacy by the enemies of Christ in the course of the conflict that would usher in the new age. But later millenarian groups, including some of the more radical Spiritual Franciscans, began to see in the Papacy itself the heart of opposition to a truly spiritual Church, and this idea, identifying Rome with the whore of Babylon (Revelation 17) and the Pope with Antichrist, was to have a powerful future at the time of the Reformation.[22]

A Joachite Franciscan group, for instance, identified the Holy Roman Emperor Frederick II (1194–1250) as Antichrist; and during the Protestant Reformations and beyond, the connection surfaced in distinctively anti-papal polemics.

20. Cited in Pelikan, *The Christian Tradition*, 3:302.
21. Cited in Brian Hebblethwaite, *The Christian Hope* (Basingstoke: Marshall and Morgan, 1984), 69.
22. Hebblethwaite, *The Christian Hope*, 69.

According to Joachim, the age of the Son would cease after a conflict between two rival popes, one of whom was Antichrist while the other would use new religious orders to launch a mission to pagans, Jews, and Muslims (based on Joachim's interpretation of Rev. 14:6). Following that, the Antichrist would be killed and the devil bound. Joachim understood the free, spiritual, and glorious third age to be both a missionary era and an era of the purification of the church and society, in which the spirit of the gospel as freedom and love would be lived out in harmony. In fact, the obsolete hierarchy of the ecclesiastical institution would be replaced by a new religious order of spiritual men, the Order of the Just, who would oversee the church. Joachim predicted further that there would continue to be resistance to this work, so that the spiritual peace and unity on earth would not be universally complete. Distant people would be in league with the devil prior to the *parousia* and the final judgment.

Numerous works purporting to be from Joachim appeared, especially with the crucial year of 1260 approaching. In 1260 and again in 1263, councils held under the leadership of the Archbishop of Arles echoed the judgment made by the Council of Trent in 1215 in condemning Joachim's ideas on the Trinity. Millenarian groups such as the panentheist Amalricians; the radically theopolitically egalitarian Dulcinians, who believed that the period since Emperor Constantine I and Pope Sylvester I constituted a decline due to the ambitions and wealth of church leaders; and the spiritually egalitarian and individualistic Brethren of the Free Spirit were all condemned and persecuted. Even so, "the idea of a total renewal and cleansing of this earth persisted."[23] It emerged particularly in the National Socialist imagery for its new order of imperial governance as constituting the Third Reich or third realm.

Reformation Apocalyptic

Martin Luther (1483–1546)

As we have seen, in the Middle Ages, under the influence of Gregorian reform and Joachimite historicism, concern about the corruption of the church had led to a number of forms of historicized expectation of a millennium to come. According to Joachim, the age of the priests, of the church, was about

---

23. Hans Schwarz, *Eschatology* (Grand Rapids: Eerdmans, 2000), 327.

to give way to reform and the age of universal love. This expectation was only intensified by the crises that beset the turbulent fourteenth and fifteenth centuries: the Black Death; the Wars of the Roses and the Hundred Years' War; a number of famines; the Western Schism; and various popular uprisings. By the beginning of the sixteenth century, the Holy Roman Empire and the Roman Catholic Church were in various states of instability. It was the Western Schism (1378–1415), in which two popes, one in Rome and another in Avignon, contested for authority, "that gave particular impetus to chiliasm [literal millennialism]. . . . Since 1378 it had seemed evident that the Church of the priests must be in its final throes."[24] Various reformist agendas, such as those of the Hussites and Wycliffe, had begun to emerge throughout Europe.

Martin Luther is perhaps most famous for his role in instigating the Protestant Reformation with his 1517 "Ninety-five Theses" nailed to the door of All Saints Church in Wittenberg. However, it is important to note that Luther did not begin with the intent of breaking away from the Roman Catholic Church. Posting theses in this way was standard medieval academic practice, not the dramatic act it is often taken to be by contemporary representations—not least Eric Till's film *Luther* (2003). Luther was looking to provoke an academic debate concerning the practices of the selling of indulgences, certificates sold by the church to lessen a loved one's time in purgatory.

Much of Luther's career thereafter was fueled by controversy, and because of this many of his writings are responses to particular occasions. Unlike John Calvin, who wrote his *Institutes of the Christian Religion* in order to collate his theological learning, Luther's thought is often scattered, and so his understanding of particular doctrinal loci is often stated polemically. For instance, one might construe the practice of selling indulgences to be eschatologically significant in that the nature of divine judgment, grace, and purgatory are all immediately in question. Yet, much of the consequent debate concerned the nature of church authority. Sylvester Mazzolini (court theologian of Pope Leo X) was asked to produce a response to Luther, which was entitled *A Dialogue against Martin Luther's Presumptuous Theses concerning the Power of the Pope*. Luther responded by trying to keep the focus on the theological problem of indulgences, to no avail. Johann Tetzl, a prominent preacher, and Johannes Eck, Luther's friend at the University of Ingolstadt, accused Luther of heresy. A papal bull was issued by Leo X in 1520, which finally condemned Luther's teaching against indulgences. Yet,

---

24. Heiko A. Oberman, *Luther: Man between God and the Devil*, trans. Eileen Walliser-Schwarbart (New Haven: Yale University Press, 1989), 60.

all of this focused on Luther's challenge of papal authority, not the strictly theological question of indulgences.

These political issues were not without their eschatological significance, however, as Luther well knew. In fact, much of his polemical language sounded distinctively apocalyptic notes. In the very title of his 1520 text *The Babylonian Captivity of the Church*, Luther invoked images of exile, the Antichrist, Rome, and an eschatological freedom. The church, for Luther, had become captive to "popish lies." Far from the radical individualist he is often depicted as, Luther was deeply concerned with the church and its ability to be itself under conditions of exile.[25] Because the church was in Babylonian captivity, the inference drawn was that the pope was indeed functioning as the Antichrist. The visible church was *not* the eschatologically disclosed invisible church. Luther would not shy away from this language as his career continued.

This vision of the political situation was predicated upon Luther's sharp distinction between the old and the new aeons.[26] This is illustrated nowhere more clearly than in his distinction between the "theology of the Cross" and the "theology of glory" in the 1518 *Heidelberg Disputation*. Here Luther draws a sharp contrast between theologians who think the glory of God is seen in the manifest power of often abusive ecclesial institutions, thereby confusing evil for good, and those who see the glory of God in the suffering of Christ.[27] It is the cross that discloses the things of God, not the glorious vestments of power that array the Roman Church. Luther then distinguishes between two aeons on this basis, and "this rupture between the ages gave shape to Luther's life and work."[28] God is the God who interrupts our sinful modes of being in the world with the radical suffering that is at the heart of the cross. All theological language, all our modes of being in the world, must be taken to judgment at the cross. In this way, the rupture between the old and the new in Luther leads him to cast the Christian life itself in apocalyptic terms.

25. This reading of Luther's individualism has its roots in the nineteenth century's leading Luther interpreter, Theodosius Harnack, who depicted Luther as a progenitor of modern humanity. See Harnack, *Luthers Theologie mit besonderer Beziehung auf seine Versöhnungs- und Erlösungslehre* [Luther's Theology with Special Reference to His Doctrines of Salvation and Redemption], 2 vols. (Erlangen, 1862).

26. Oswald Bayer, *Martin Luther's Theology: A Contemporary Interpretation*, trans. Thomas H. Trapp (Grand Rapids: Eerdmans, 2008).

27. Martin Luther, *Heidelberg Disputation*, in *Luther's Works*, vol. 34: *Career of the Reformer IV*, trans. Lewis W. Spitz, general ed. Helmut T. Lehmann (Minneapolis: Fortress, 1960).

28. Bayer, *Martin Luther's Theology*, 1.

Baptism is the marker of this break with the old, and "ethical advances can come only in the return to one's baptism."[29] Only then can we repent and return to this moment when God interrupts the old with the new.

Later in his career tensions developed with more radical reformers, particularly with Thomas Müntzer, for whom Luther had little theological time, over the political implications of the break with papal corruption. Müntzer became one of the key figures in the German Peasants' War (1524–1525), encouraging peasants to take up arms against the aristocracy. We will speak about Müntzer more in the next section, but here we will note that Luther was deeply troubled by his call to violent revolt. In "Against the Robbing and Murdering Hordes of Peasants" (1525) Luther protested the use of violence, suggesting that this was contrary to the gospel and those using violence in the name of the gospel were really doing the work of Satan. Again, he sounds apocalyptic notes: "I believe also that the devil foresees the judgment day, that he undertakes such an unheard-of measure; as if he said, 'It is the last and therefore it shall be the worst; I'll stir up the dregs and knock the very bottom out.'"[30] We can see here how Luther located this very real and immediate political conflict within the context of a cosmic battle between God and the devil. Müntzer and his followers were, for Luther, unwittingly doing the work of the devil by perpetrating violence upon their persecutors.

Luther's vision of what we call the "last things"—resurrection, the after-life, etc.—was in many ways quite uncontroversial. In his commentary on 1 Corinthians 15, Luther describes the resurrection body as still gendered but says the accompanying institution of marriage is done away with. Similarly, all rank and order are abolished in the new order, and the body will suffer no physical ill. The body remains corporeal, but it is transfigured in some way beyond description. The body as it is in its present state remains unfit for heaven, but it will in the end be transfigured into a spiritual body.[31]

Toward the end of his life Luther indulged in some speculation regarding the end of history, but this was always shrouded by the assertion that we know not the day nor the hour of the Lord's return. What is important to note about Luther's eschatological thought, however, is the way in which the imminent arrival of the end of the old history, and the beginning of the new history, is present in the decisive break that is the cross. This means that

29. Bayer, *Martin Luther's Theology*, 12.

30. "Against the Robbing and Murdering Hordes of Peasants," in *The Reformation Sourcebook*, ed. Michael W. Bruening (Toronto: University of Toronto Press, 2017), 86.

31. David P. Scaer, "Luther's Concept of the Resurrection in His Commentary on 1 Corinthians 15," *Concordia Theological Quarterly* 47 (1983): 209–24.

Luther can cast the battle for the human heart between God and the devil as an eschatological battle as we attempt to inhabit a cruciform life. It is only with reference to the apocalyptic breaking in of God's new life in the cross that human life can be understood and lived. Any attempt to evade the cross is an attempt to save oneself through works; it is to evade the catastrophic power of God's judgment and grace. Luther saw this in the papacy's abuse of power but also in the Peasants' War. Both were the result of human effort to inaugurate a human vision of the good and the good life. The theologian of the cross, however, can apprehend divine action only through suffering and the cross.

Thomas Müntzer (1489–1525)

The radical reformations were inherently apocalyptic movements in the way they called down judgment on clergy and on social and political institutions, while promising an imminent final judgment and vindication of the elect. Exemplary among these figures is Thomas Müntzer, a contemporary of Luther. Müntzer's legacy is diverse and scattered. His thought responded to particular occasions rather than answering grand systematic questions—he was a preacher and self-styled apocalyptic prophet rather than a university professor like Luther. There was a consistent motor to his theological engine, however—that is, the belief that the last days were upon him.

Driving this were two things fundamental to Müntzer's thought. First was the deep sense of betrayal by the clergy who abused their power in order to economically and politically oppress the poor laity. The clergy were, for him, "a plague on the people." A variety of phrases were used to describe the clergy: "'Diarrhea-makers' . . . and 'whore-mongers' . . . who possess a 'whore's brazenness' . . . and are 'money hungry rogues' . . ."[32] The commoners, on the other hand, "a poor, poor, pitiable mass . . . get no justice either from God or from man."[33] Second, Müntzer spent a lot of time early in his career reading the German mystics. While Luther was studying scholastic theology and philosophy alongside the mystics, Müntzer read them alone. In this way his reformation was very different from Luther's, for he was

32. Michael G. Baylor, "Introduction," in *Revelation and Revolution: Basic Writings of Thomas Müntzer*, trans. and ed. Michael G. Baylor (Bethlehem, PA: Lehigh University Press, 1993), 17.

33. Thomas Müntzer, *The Prague Protest* (hereafter *PP*), in Baylor, *Revelation and Revolution*, 57. Page references are given in parentheses in the text.

not interested in the recovery of the Scriptures as a source of religious authority. Rather, he was intent on establishing a form of religious interiority and experience that precedes the Scriptures. Hence, Müntzer's reformation was "radical" in its appeal to inward experience rather than to an external authority. It is only those who have suffered, the elect, who have the ability to attain this inwardness.

Müntzer considered Luther to have co-opted the German princes for his own ends in the way he constructed his theological politics.[34] Luther treated the princes with great deference and rejected any hint of violent revolt. Müntzer, however, saw in Luther's distinction between law and gospel a ready-made excuse for authorities to commit violence, for in that distinction faith was won without a price, without the inward transformation and suffering Müntzer saw as preparation for the elect. Luther, in his work on the two kingdoms, suggested that subjects must be obedient to the law of the ruling authorities. Müntzer thought that this provided the people with no room to resist the harsh conditions in which they found themselves, while Luther's doctrine of grace let abusive princes off the hook. Müntzer's late polemics show the tensions among the reformers themselves, as he identifies Luther and the princes as the locus of apocalyptic chaos. For Müntzer, Luther was "the pope of Wittenberg."

In July-November 1521 Müntzer stayed in Prague, preaching in various churches and writing *The Prague Protest*, in which he designates himself as the successor to the Bohemian reformer Jan Hus, who was burned at the stake as a heretic, and calls down judgment upon the authorities. He was placed under house arrest by the authorities upon the publication of this work, and he was finally exiled from the city amid reports of crowds attempting to stone him.[35]

Müntzer begins his document by throwing doubt upon the veracity of the faith of the clergy and of Luther, a "pseudospiritual monk" (*PP*, 54). They "cannot say anything about the foundation of the faith in even its smallest point" (*PP*, 54). The ordinary people, then, have been left to "elevate themselves spiritually." They can do this because of their suffering. Müntzer turns again and again to the benefits of suffering for the spiritual life and the dire consequences for those who live lives of comfort: "The clergy have never

---

34. Thomas Müntzer, *Highly Provoked Defence*, in Baylor, *Revelation and Revolution*, 139-54.

35. Eric W. Gritsch, *Thomas Müntzer: A Tragedy of Errors* (Minneapolis: Fortress, 2006), 42.

been able to discover, nor will they ever, the beneficial tribulations and useful abyss that the providential spirit needs as it empties itself" (*PP*, 55). This language echoes the great German mystic who influenced both Müntzer and Luther, Johannes Tauler. He spoke continually about the need to empty oneself so as to be filled up by God.[36] For Müntzer, those who already suppose themselves to be full, and in no need of suffering, have no room for God. "Unbelievers can and will not empty themselves" (*PP*, 56).

The distinction between the elect and the reprobate is hardened throughout the text as Müntzer insists further upon the validity of his experiential revelations. He draws on the images of the key of David (Rev. 3:7), by which the gospel is opened for the elect and locked away from the damned, and Ezekiel's unlocking of historical events in order to legitimize his own revelations. The Scriptures, then, simply bear witness to something already inwardly established by a revelation. The heart is "the paper and parchment on which God does not write with ink, but rather writes the true holy Scripture with his living fingers about which the external Bible truly testifies." Scholars and monks are excluded from this inward revelation by virtue of their fixation upon externalities, and so they "suffer no tribulation of faith in the spirit of the fear of God, so they are on their way to the fiery lake, where the false prophets will be tormented with the Antichrist for ever and ever, Amen" (*PP*, 55).

There is a clear logic in Müntzer's thought: if one truly has faith, then this is born of suffering. However, if one does not suffer, then one cannot have faith. Tribulation and suffering serve to separate the wheat from the weeds (*PP*, 55). It is important to note that Müntzer understands this parable to be fulfilled in the time of his writing. In the original scriptural text the disciples are warned not to pull up the weeds, for they might risk pulling up wheat (Matt. 13:29). Judgment takes place only in the last days. Müntzer sees his moment as the moment of the eschatological harvest, when God throws the weeds into the fire. The risk the disciples faced, of pulling up wheat accidentally, is no longer an issue for Müntzer, for he can see "as though it were midday." The implication of all of this is that Müntzer himself, and the community that rallies to him, is privy to an apocalyptic revelation of the end. Immediately prior to appealing for others' support he states,

Oh her, how ripe are the corn so apparent! Oh ho, how mushy the elect have become! The time of the harvest is at hand! *Thus God himself has appointed me for his harvest. I have made my sickle sharp, for my*

36. *Johannes Tauler: Sermons*, trans. Maria Shrady (New York: Paulist, 1985), 35–40.

thoughts are zealous for the truth and my lips, skin, hands, hair, soul, body, and my life all damn the unbelievers. (*PP*, 59, emphasis added)

Throughout *The Prague Protest* Müntzer casts himself as an eschatological prophet who will lead the elect in their final charge against the dark forces at work in the world. This culminates at the end of the document with a warning and apocalyptic prediction: "Whoever despises such warnings as these is already, now, in the hands of the Turks. After this raging conflagration, the true Antichrist will personally reign, the radical opposite of Christ. And shortly after this, Christ will give to his elect the kingdom of this world for all eternity" (*PP*, 60). This prediction gave rise to suspicions that Müntzer was a Joachimite, which he denied. However, in spite of his rejection of Joachim's scheme, clearly he believed he was living in the midst of the last days, and he understood himself as their herald.

Müntzer is perhaps most famous for his role in the 1525 Peasants' War, in which those around him rose up against the princes and the clergy. Just two years earlier, however, he had warned against violent revolution in an *Open Letter to the Brothers at Stohlberg*. Only when we "don the jewels of the king," the knowledge of God, "will the whole world be confirmed as the assembly place of the elect, so the world obtains a Christian governance that no sack of gunpowder will be able to overthrow."[37] The true kingdom of God begins "with genuine pleasure when the elect first see what God lets them discover in themselves, through his action, in the experience of the spirit."[38] Both in the earlier apocalyptic appeal to revolution, embodied in the 1521 *Prague Protest*, and in the more temperate 1523 appeal to peace, we see the same crucial formulation of interiority and suffering. The suffering of the elect is constantly a sign of the last days.

When revolution finally arrived, it was quickly put down, and Müntzer was beheaded outside the walls of Mülhausen on May 27, 1525. The sixteenth century had both historically and theologically become deeply embroiled in a sense of apocalyptic urgency. The world was changing, and it was changing very quickly, regardless of whether one were Catholic, Lutheran, Calvinist, or radical. The Reformation had set fire to Europe, and it appeared that the last days of the Roman Catholic Church as it had been, if not the world, were at hand.

37. Müntzer, *Open Letter to the Brothers at Stohlberg*, in Baylor, *Revelation and Revolution*, 62.

38. Müntzer, *Open Letter to the Brothers at Stohlberg*, in Baylor, *Revelation and Revolution*, 61.

Dispensationalism

We have seen that, for Joachim, theology and the emergence of historical consciousness were deeply implicated in one another. For Joachimites the different ages of history were understood as a product of the different divine actors on the stage of history. However, Reformed Protestants in the seventeenth century began to speak of history as divided by different covenants. These Federal Calvinists, broadly speaking, divided history into three covenants: works, grace, and redemption. A prime example of this division of history is found in the work of Johannes Cocceus. For him, the covenant of works was the time of Israel's dealings with God in the Hebrew Bible, where obedience to the law was the covenantal obligation of the creature. The covenant of grace runs through the entire history of salvation, both before and after the historical birth of Christ, and is predicated upon Christ's eventual assumption of the burden of the covenant of works on behalf of the creature, first as promise, then as actuality and memory. The covenant of redemption is made between the Father and the Son, whereby the Son agrees to take upon himself the guilt of the human creatures and to atone for them; the Father then agrees to raise Christ from the dead into imperishable life. This covenant is internal to God's own life. One might interpret these different covenants in different ways in relation to "salvation history," and later generations of Reformed theologians did. One might see them as different historical epochs, or one might see them as running alongside one another throughout history. Whatever the case may be, God's dealings with the creature are understood in historicized terms. Indeed, God's own decision to covenant God's self with the creature is a historical decision.[39] Covenant becomes the organizing principle of theology and history.

While covenant theology became a dominant mode of thinking about the history of salvation through the seventeenth and eighteenth centuries, dispensationalism emerged as something of a resistance to this understanding of salvation history within conservative Protestantism.[40] Yet, it main-

---

39. This became an issue in the controversy at the Synod of Dort over infralapsarian and supralapsarian covenants. In the former, God enters into a covenant with God's self and the creature after the historical fall, in the latter, the covenant precedes the historical fall. In both instances God foresees the fall.

40. This was the case particularly as concerns over the last days and Israel's centrality to them emerged with political gusto in the mid-twentieth century. See Stephen D. O'Leary, *Arguing the Apocalypse: A Theory of Millennial Rhetoric* (Oxford: Oxford University Press, 1998), 172-93.

tained the same concern with theology as a way of schematizing the unfolding history of salvation.

Dispensationalism refers to a movement in theology that divides history into as many as seven different periods or dispensations: innocence, prior to Adam's fall; conscience, from Adam to Noah; government, from Noah to Abraham; the Patriarchs, from Abraham to Moses; the time of the law, from Moses to Christ; the age of the church, or grace; and the millennium to come.[41] The movement began with the Anglo-Irishman John Nelson Darby (1800–1882), who promoted his teaching concerning the six dispensations of history among the Plymouth Brethren in the 1830s.

The American Charles Ingerson Scofield (1843–1921) further popularized and extended Darby's teaching through the publication of the *Scofield Reference Bible*, a study Bible with notes intended to aid the reader in interpreting the text. This proved an effective means of promoting dispensational teaching through evangelicals' devotion to the Scriptures. For Scofield the division of history into dispensations is intended to convey the different situation humanity faces before God in each dispensation. Each dispensation "ends in judgement, marking [humanity's] utter failure in every dispensation." According to Scofield we currently live in the sixth dispensation, at the end of which will come judgment. At the end of this period the first thing to happen will be the "descent of the Lord from heaven, when sleeping saints will be raised and, together with believers then living, caught up 'to meet the Lord in the air: and so shall we ever be with the Lord' (I Thess. 4:16–17)." This is commonly known as the rapture. Once the saints have left the scene, the world will be left to face "the brief period called 'the great tribulation.'" After this period of judgment, in which the bowls of wrath will be poured out on the face of the earth, Christ will return again to reign for one thousand years before the final loosing of Satan and the final judgment. Further, because each of the dispensations is bracketed from the next by judgment, dispensationalists maintain a distinction between Israel and the church. This has had political consequences that we will discuss momentarily.

This scheme has been rethought by more recent, progressive dispensationalists who are concerned to ensure that each of the dispensations is not thought of as bracketed entirely from the next; rather, there is a progression

---

41. C. I. Scofield, *Rightly Dividing the Word of Truth*, chapter 2. https://www.bible believers.com/scofield/scofield_rightly02.html (accessed January 26, 2017). Quotations in this paragraph are from this source. Darby initially omitted the first dispensation, which Scofield then includes.

within the dispensations. They have also attempted to further refine the language of covenant and dispensation so as to overcome some of the barriers to conversation between these two camps in Protestant theology.[42]

Dispensationalism has subsequently influenced figures such as Hal Lindsey, whose *Late Great Planet Earth* drew comparisons between scriptural texts and current events in the late 1960s to the early 1970s. His book went on to be adapted into a film directed by Orson Welles. Tim LaHaye, the author of the popular *Left Behind* book series, which has also been adapted to the cinema, is also heavily influenced by Scofield. In Lindsey's 1970 text *Late Great Planet Earth*, the suggestion was that the world would end within forty years of 1948, the date of the Arab-Israeli war. Lindsey had made calculations on the basis of this event and his interpretation of Hebrew prophecy.[43] This was, needless to say, a rather bleak outlook on the state of political life in the very near future, given the anticipated period of judgment. As Lindsey's teacher, John F. Walvoord, stated, "The world today is like a stage being set for a great drama. . . . Since the stage is set for this dramatic climax of the age, it must mean that Christ's coming for his own is very near."[44]

However, throughout the 1970s and early 1980s, a new optimism emerged on the Christian right, first with the election of Jimmy Carter, and then with Ronald Reagan, who was politically and theologically sensitive to dispensationalism. In 1982, with the end of the world looming, Lindsey published *1980's: Countdown to Armageddon*. Here, however, Lindsey's rhetoric had changed. With renewed confidence supported by a sympathetic president, we see the emergence of a convergence of the Reaganite Republican political agenda, patriotism, and Lindsey's apocalypticism: "We must actively take on the responsibility of being a citizen and a member of God's family. We need to get active electing officials who will not only reflect the Bible's morality in government but will shape domestic and foreign policies to protect our country and way of life."[45]

Where previously we had been helpless on the stage of history, now participation in politics had become central to the apocalyptic narrative of the

42. Darrel Bock and Craig A. Blaising, *Progressive Dispensationalism* (Grand Rapids: Baker Academic, 2000).

43. Hal Lindsey with Carole C. Carlson, *The Late Great Planet Earth* (Grand Rapids: Zondervan, 1970).

44. John W. Walvoord, *Armageddon, Oil and the Middle East Crisis* (Grand Rapids: Zondervan, 1990), 228. Quoted in O'Leary, *Arguing the Apocalypse*, 176-77.

45. Hal Lindsey, *The 1980's: Countdown to Armageddon* (San Francisco: Westgate, 1982). Quoted in O'Leary, *Arguing the Apocalypse*, 176-77.

new Christian right. Military, political, and economic support for the state of Israel became a fundamental spiritual task, which has manifested itself in American foreign policy for at least the last thirty years. Dispensationalism has managed to wed apocalyptic fervor to a narrative of national destiny in an unprecedentedly successful manner.

Because of his catastrophic vision of the future, when Lindsey envisions the last things, he envisions not a renewed earth, but the destruction of the earth. Heaven is, then, an escape from this world after being called into the clouds. Conversely, hell is likened to "exactly what happens to those who are in a thermonuclear blast."[46] It is the eternal conscious torment of those who find themselves suffering the wrath of God.

Liberalism and the Return of Apocalyptic

The main interest of influential German biblical scholarship of the mid-nineteenth century was the nature of Jesus's consciousness of his mission. While chapter 2 will discuss the genesis of modernity and the types of eschatologies it spawned, and the significance of the implications of these eschatologies for Christian hope, for now it is worth indicating that their impact contributed to a burgeoning sense of Jesus as a moral teacher and exemplar whose message about the kingdom of God provided the rational moral norm for individuals and their societies. This theological sensibility itself built on the work of scholars focusing on the "liberal lives of Jesus." These scholars created reconstructed narratives of Jesus's life grounded in psychological and historical analysis of the Gospel narratives. This approach largely interiorized eschatological themes in the individual's consciousness, making the theme of the kingdom of God little more than the moral association of people. Adolf von Harnack announced, "The kingdom comes by coming to the individual, by entering into his soul and laying hold of it. True, the kingdom of God is the rule of God; but it is the rule of the holy God in the hearts of individuals."[47] For Harnack, this meant that talk of the kingdom does not properly involve "a question of angels and demons, thrones and principalities, but" has to do with "God and the soul, the soul and its God."[48] Accordingly, just

46. Quoted in Christopher Morse, *The Difference Heaven Makes: Rehearing the Gospel as Good News* (London: T&T Clark, 2010), 36.

47. Adolf von Harnack, *What Is Christianity?*, trans. Thomas Bailey Saunders (New York: Harper & Row, 1957), 56.

48. Harnack, *What Is Christianity?*, 56.

prior to the outbreak of World War I, Ernst Troeltsch announced, "The eschatological bureau is closed these days."[49]

This situation changed remarkably soon afterwards, however, so much so that "eschatology" was to become one of the most fashionable words in twentieth-century academic theology, and perhaps dominated the imagination of twentieth-century theology more than most other themes and topics. Picking up Troeltsch's image, Hans Urs von Balthasar declared that the eschatological office had now been working overtime since the turn of the nineteenth into the twentieth century.[50] Among the reasons for this were the contributions to biblical studies by the Germans Johannes Weiss (1863–1914) and Albert Schweitzer (1875–1965). Textbooks often speak of their work by coupling them together as leading a "rediscovery" of eschatology.[51] But stating things in that way is not entirely helpful, since it misses the interest in eschatological matters, especially apocalyptic ones, among a number of groups and writers up to that time. On the other hand, the effect of their work on academic biblical and theological studies was certainly pronounced, forcing twentieth-century scholars to take eschatology seriously in a way that has had an impact on the mainstream church traditions and academia.

The first edition of a short book by Weiss, professor of New Testament at Göttingen, in 1892 promoted Jesus's proclamation of the kingdom of God to the central place in New Testament study. After providing a comparison of the Gospels with Jewish apocalyptic literature (such as Daniel, the Assumption of Moses, and the book of Enoch), it argued that Jesus's conception of the kingdom contradicted those that characterized the portrayals of Protestant liberal scholarship, portrayals that had "completely stripped away the original eschatological-apocalyptic meaning of the idea" of the kingdom of God.[52] To begin with, for Weiss's Jesus, the kingdom was "always the messianic kingdom," and it was still entirely future (rather than something interiorized in the believer), even if it was near (*JPKG*, 133). From there, Weiss demonstrated that Jesus's preaching was not just that of "the fatherhood of God and the brotherhood of man"; it was, on the contrary, thoroughly eschatological—it proclaimed God's imminent in-breaking from beyond in order to abolish the old world and create a new one in which Jesus himself, as

---

49. Cited in F. L. Polak, *The Image of the Future* (Oxford: Elsevier-Phaidon, 1973), 243.

50. Hans Urs von Balthasar, *Essays in Theology*, vol. 2: *Word and Redemption*, trans. A. V. Littledale (New York: Herder and Herder, 1965), 147.

51. So, for example, Schwarz, *Eschatology*, 108.

52. Johannes Weiss, *Jesus' Proclamation of the Kingdom of God*, trans. R. H. Hiers and D. L. Holland (Philadelphia: Fortress, 1971), 114. Hereafter *JPKG*.

the Messiah, would be the King within the eschatological reign of God. "By virtue of his baptismal experience, Jesus reached the religious conviction that he had been chosen to be Judge and Ruler in the Kingdom of God. . . . The messianic consciousness of Jesus, as expressed in the name Son of man, also participates in the thoroughly transcendental and apocalyptic character of Jesus' idea of the Kingdom of God and cannot be dissociated from it" (*JPKG*, 128–29). This means that the kingdom of God in Jesus's preaching was not a continuous development of existing factors in human history, or indeed of any and all human work. Instead, it was understood as a future cataclysmic act of the God who intervenes in human history and catastrophically brings with it the end of the world. "The disciples were to pray for the coming of the Kingdom, but men could do nothing to establish it" (*JPKG*, 129).

Shaped by this eschatological sensibility, and following that of John the Baptist, Jesus engaged after his baptism in preparing his audience for the coming of the kingdom. Jesus was concerned with the kind of repentance that people would show in the brief period left before the kingdom's coming. Although the kingdom's coming would be a future cataclysmic act of God, its shadow had already been cast across the world by the presence of Jesus. Gradually Jesus came to realize that its arrival had somehow been delayed by human guilt. As a result, he determined that only his own death at the hands of guilty people would become the means of expiating guilt and causing the kingdom of God to arrive, established in the coming of the exalted Son of Man on the clouds, within his generation's lifetime. Weiss then explained the transformation of Jesus's historic message at the hands of his supporters when the kingdom did not arrive as expected. Drawing on ideas and beliefs in the Hellenistic world, Jesus's followers transformed Christianity into the worship of a divine Christ who would return in judgment at the end of time.

"The effect of the book was like that of a brick hurled at a plate-glass window. The book was so offensive because liberal theology had a bad conscience about its suppression of Jesus' eschatology. . . . Thanks to Weiss, the liberal emperor was seen to have no clothes."[53] The outcry over the study was considerable, and Weiss caved in under the pressure, admitting that while his study expressed the "*historical* truth" it was not a contribution to the ongoing truthfulness of Christianity. Thus, after his sally into the no-man's-land of eschatology, Weiss, a former student of Albrecht Ritschl and his son-in-law, returned again at once to the liberal picture of the moral significance of Jesus

---

53. Benedict Viviano, "Eschatology and the Quest for the Historical Jesus," in *The Oxford Handbook of Eschatology*, ed. Jerry L. Walls (Oxford: Oxford University Press, 2008), 79.

he had articulated earlier: "That which is universally valid in Jesus' preaching is not his idea of the kingdom of God, but that of the religious and ethical fellowship of the children of God" (*JPKG*, 135). Weiss therefore drew a sharp contrast between the world-ending message of the historical Jesus and his contemporary theological significance for which "we do hope to be gathered with the church of Jesus Christ into the heavenly 'Kingdom'" (*JPKG*, 135).

Weiss's book paved the way for the celebrated work of 1906, *The Quest of the Historical Jesus*, as well as its precursor of 1901, *The Mystery of the Kingdom of God*, composed by the Alsatian polymath Albert Schweitzer. Both of these books echoed a good many of Weiss's themes, although apparently Schweitzer reached his "consistent eschatology" independently from Weiss.

His concern, like Weiss's, was to complicate and disrupt the liberal domestication of Jesus's apocalyptic sensibility. Taking aim at the work on the "historical Jesus" done from Reimarus to Wrede, the *Quest* book argues that the portrait of Jesus as an ethical teacher was essentially a creation of rationalistic liberalism and that scholars had been writing lives of Jesus that mirrored their own values.[54] Scholars, he noted, produced portraits of Jesus that they personally found appealing. For non-Christians Jesus turned out to be a fraud, whereas for Christians Jesus believed and valued precisely the things the scholars did. Liberal scholars had modernized Jesus so as to make him relevant to their time. However, this entailed that little about Jesus appeared to be specifically Jewish. Schweitzer regarded these liberal scholars as having gone badly wrong in categorically failing to appreciate the radical but strange eschatological message of Jesus.

In his earlier book, he spent time unpacking the messianic consciousness of Jesus from the time of his baptism and the sense of his role in the coming of the kingdom of God as the messianic Suffering Servant and the forthcoming eschatological Son of Man. He understood Jesus's apocalyptic message to involve only the expectation of imminent events and the announcement of a preparatory or "interim ethics" that is "oriented entirely by the expected supernatural consummation."[55] These had to do with the global catastrophe through which the kingdom of God would break into worldly reality in order to thoroughly transform it, and the coming or *parousia* of the Son of Man "upon the clouds of heaven for judgment" (*MKG*, 191). Once

54. Albert Schweitzer, *The Quest of the Historical Jesus: A Critical Study of Its Progress from Reimarus to Wrede*, 3rd ed., trans. W. Montgomery (London: Adam & Charles Black, 1954). Hereafter *QHJ*.

55. Albert Schweitzer, *The Mystery of the Kingdom of God*, trans. Walter Lowrie (London: Adam & Charles Black, 1956), 55, 100. Hereafter *MKG*.

it was clear that the kingdom had not arrived on the beheading of John the Baptist, Jesus realized that he would have to suffer death as well. Therefore, "Jesus . . . sets his death in temporal-causal connection with the eschatological dawning of the Kingdom" (*MKG*, 80). As he put it in his later book: "In the knowledge that He is the coming Son of Man [Jesus] lays hold of the wheel of the world to set it moving on that last revolution which is to bring all ordinary history to a close. It refuses to turn, and He throws Himself upon it. Then it does turn; and crushes Him" (*QHJ*, 370-71).

What appealed to Schweitzer was a certain heroic status of Jesus, even though in the end Jesus was "a kind of religious fanatic who was deceived by his own ideas."[56] The global realization of the apocalyptic events anticipated by Jesus did not transpire, even on the death of Jesus. Consequently, at least in terms of what Schweitzer considered to be most theologically interesting and relevant in Jesus's ministry, Schweitzer's hopes were inconsistent with what he understood to be the thrust of the historical Jesus's own demands. Theologically, Schweitzer had little eschatological sensibility. As one commentator summarizes, "Since the kingdom had not come when Jesus expected it, our ethics cannot be derived from Jesus' ethics."[57] Christianity, Schweitzer maintained, could never simply return to this strange, enigmatic, eschatological figure of Jesus.[58]

However, this segregation of the apocalyptic historical Jesus from the ethically inspiring Christ was to change radically in the theological environment after World War I. Paraphrasing Franz Overbeck, Jürgen Moltmann described the change this way: "The recognition of the eschatological character of early Christianity made it clear that the automatically accepted idea of a harmonious synthesis between Christianity and culture was a lie."[59] To this we now turn.

---

56. Schwarz, *Eschatology*, 113.

57. Schwarz, *Eschatology*, 112.

58. Scholars such as Martin Werner (1887-1964) claimed that the whole development of Christian dogma was the de-eschatologizing result of what amounted to a sense of crisis over the delay of the imminently expected *parousia* and eschaton. Martin Werner, *The Formation of Christian Dogma: An Historical Study of Its Problem*, trans. S. G. F. Brandon (New York: Harper, 1957), 47, 71-72.

59. Jürgen Moltmann, *Theology of Hope: On the Ground and the Implications of a Christian Eschatology*, trans. Margaret Kohl (London: SCM, 1967), 37.

Weimar Apocalypticism

Key to understanding the resurgence in apocalyptic tropes in the early twentieth century is the Swiss-German Reformed theologian, pastor, and political activist Karl Barth (to whom we will return in chapter 4). Barth gained theological notoriety after his 1919 commentary on Paul's epistle to the Romans, *Der Römerbrief*, which, as one reader remarked, "dropped like a bomb on the playground of the theologians."[60] Barth had been educated by some of the leading lights in contemporary theology, notably the liberal historical theologian—and friend of the Kaiser—Adolf von Harnack and the renowned systematic theologian Wilhelm Hermann. However, following the outbreak of war in 1914 and the horrors thereby unleashed, Barth found himself in intense and sustained theological disagreement with the political positions of his teachers.

On October 4, 1914, both Harnack and Hermann were among ninety-three German intellectuals who signed the infamous "Manifesto of the Ninety-Three," a letter of support of the Kaiser and his war effort. The letter concludes, "Have faith in us! Believe, that we shall carry on this war to the end as a civilized nation, to whom the legacy of a Goethe, a Beethoven, and a Kant is just as sacred as its own hearths and homes."[61] As a Swiss citizen Barth remained an outsider, which may have helped his perception as it became clear to him that his teachers had fallen prey to an ideology of national progress. Barth developed a distinct distaste for any theological outlook whose success was contingent upon a secular political program.

Barth eventually grew dissatisfied with the first edition of his Romans commentary, which maintained historicist tendencies, given its use of Hegelian themes. He authored a second edition much more indebted to the work of Søren Kierkegaard, Friedrich Nietzsche, Franz Overbeck, and Martin Luther, among others. Here Barth developed language that became common currency among the "Dialectical School" of which he was a part, that of *Krisis* (crisis or divine judgment).[62] This language was expressed in

---

60. Karl Adam, "Die Theologie der Krisis," *Hochland* 23 (1926): 271.

61. "Manifesto of the Ninety-Three Intellectuals," https://wwi.lib.byu.edu/index.php /Manifesto_of_the_Ninety-Three_German_Intellectuals (accessed January 28, 2017).

62. The Dialectical School included figures such as Emil Brunner, Rudolf Bultmann, and Friedrich Gogarten. These young theologians were all in one way or another making a break from the prevailing, largely aristocratic and politically docile liberalism of the theological academy. It remains difficult to generalize about these figures; however, each was deeply in-

a number of striking ways. Whereas earlier historicisms had been tempted to speak of the unfolding of history as the unfolding of divine revelation, Barth spoke of revelation as a crater: "But the activity of the community is related to the Gospel only in so far as it is no more than a crater formed by the explosion of a shell and seeks to be no more than a void in which the Gospel reveals itself."[63]

Barth stood at the edge of the collapse of liberal confidence in historical progress and called a halt, with a return to apocalyptic tropes of messianism and divine revelation. His work, then, stands at the root of a renewed contemporary interest in apocalypticism and political critique, which blurs the boundaries between the theological and the philosophical, the sacred and the secular. This can be seen at work in recent theological and philosophical figures such as Slavoj Žižek, Giorgio Agamben, Stanley Hauerwas, Ernst Käsemann, and John Howard Yoder. Their work stands at the end of a long tradition of historicized apocalyptic, starting at least with Joachim in the twelfth century. European Christian and Enlightenment history came to a head with the events of World War I, events apocalyptically charged. Here we see both the durability and the flexibility of apocalyptic.

Returning briefly to where we began with Kovacs and Rowland's distinction between actualizing and decoding forms of interpretation of Revelation, we might suggest that World War I made it impossible for people like Barth to affirm any kind of historical progress after the manner of Joachim. History, and the misplaced optimism of futurist eschatologies, had become for them but rubble. If apocalyptic was to be maintained, it needed to look something more like an actualized critique of abuse of power and misplaced confidence in efforts to inaugurate utopia. This situation in Europe, however, was markedly different to that in America, where the apocalyptic imagination emerged with renewed futurist vigor in the wake of the First World War. Context remains crucial to how we understand the purpose and character of apocalyptic.

---

vested in thinking his way through the crisis of culture Germany faced in the wake of defeat in World War I.

63. Karl Barth, *The Epistle to the Romans*, trans. Edwyn C. Hoskyns (Oxford: Oxford University Press, 1936), 36.

2. *Existential*

In chapter 1 we dealt with various kinds of apocalyptic approaches to eschatology and the ways they can be construed in futurist/predictive (decoding)
or symbolic (actualizing) terms. Broadly speaking, these approaches entail
some kind of unveiling or action "from above." That is to say, divine action
and judgment are paramount. As we move into the territory of the existential
approach, we begin to deal with eschatologies that we can speak of as emerging "from below." Yet there is a great deal of variety here, and understanding
the contexts is consequently immensely important.

We shall move through three major periods in the history of theology:
the fathers, the Middle Ages, and modernity. As we move through each of
these periods we shall see that what we mean by "the existential" will have
to adapt. In particular, the way God is spoken of changes significantly under
the conditions of modernity. In both Bultmannian thought and one type of
feminist theology, with which the chapter concludes, we witness a profound
adaptation and shift in theological language. Yet, as we shall see in Hans Urs
von Balthasar's thought and another type of feminist theology, there are
moderns who prefer to maintain much of the tradition in this area, drawing
from figures such as Origen and Julian of Norwich.

Broadly speaking, then, we shall see two different kinds of existential
approaches. The Bultmannian approach emphasizes the way modern scientific accounts of history and the world preclude the mythological accounts
of divine action of the New Testament. Bultmann reshapes eschatological
assertions in terms of the existential encounter of God and human in faith.
One might see this as a way of extending Luther's vision of the apocalyptic crisis of faith. On the other hand, thinkers such as Origen, Julian, and

Balthasar speak of divine drama, of God as the great pedagogue guiding us through history, of the obscurity of God's life. History for these thinkers is a participation in God's life. This vision is maintained by Balthasar in spite of the pressures of the modern sciences, and it is significantly modified by others, such as Catherine Keller. As with the apocalyptic approach, then, the existential approach is a broad path along which we can trace another route up the mountain of Christian theological history.

Origen of Alexandria (184–253)

Origen was one of the most significant and difficult thinkers of the early Christian period. He is significant because, although it is something of an anachronistic comment, he was the fountainhead of the theology of much of what came to be the Coptic and Eastern Orthodox churches and also was hugely influential in the Latin west. He was the most significant exegete of Scripture in the patristic period. Moreover, he set the stage for much of the early Christian appropriation and criticism of philosophical sources. His thought continues to inform and inspire many of the most significant theologians of our own day.

Studies of Origen at the turn of the twentieth century were dominated by what is known as the Hellenization thesis, associated particularly with the German historical-theologian whom we met in chapter 1, Adolf von Harnack (1851–1930). This thesis posited that as Christianity moved further into the Greek world it became alienated from its most primitive concerns. The task of the historical-theologian, then, was the reconstruction of earliest Christian theology, cleansed from the corrupting influence of Greek philosophical conceptuality. Origen was for a long time understood as emblematic of this thesis; someone who was apparently manifestly concerned to accommodate Christian language to Greek philosophical categories. While this misunderstanding of Origen has its roots in much older controversies surrounding his work,[1] he became synonymous with several doctrinal anomalies. These included ideas such as the preexistence of the soul (immortal human souls descend into bodies at birth); the possibility of a second fall (after the restoration of all things, human freedom might still leave open the possibility of a new fall into alienation and sin); the subordination of the Son to the

---

1. See Rowan Williams, "Origen: Between Orthodoxy and Heresy," in *Origeniana Septima*, ed. W. A. Beinert and U. Kühneweg (Leuven: Leuven University Press, 1999), 3–14.

Father (a hierarchy is established in God's very life); and an irresistible *apokatastasis* (universal salvation) (ultimately all persons and demonic agents are determined by God to be reconciled to God's self).

In the middle of the twentieth century, the mood of European interpretation of the fathers began to change under the influence of figures associated with the *nouvelle théologie*, particularly Jean Daniélou, Henri de Lubac, and Hans Urs von Balthasar. These thinkers began to interpret Origen's use of philosophical sources as contingent upon prior theological commitments. For these readers, philosophical conceptuality provided Origen with the ability to articulate the gospel in creative ways. One of the reasons interpreters of Origen started to turn against proponents of the Hellenization thesis was because of the way they understood Origen's concept of the *Logos* (Word) of God as that which pervades all things. Balthasar suggested that what was at stake in Origen's appropriation of philosophy was not so much an alien interpolation into a pristine, historically recoverable, original gospel message as a rearticulation of the Word in his own particular location. Hence, he saw Origen's theology as less an accommodation to Platonism and more a creative rearticulation of the heart of the gospel.

Origen was, first and foremost, an interpreter of the Scriptures. In his thought, the Word is understood as that which enlivens the Scriptures, bringing them to bear again and again in an ever fresh manner. Further, the Word is the creative Word, the Word of the Father. The Word is that in which all things consist and in which they image the Father. One cannot then take flight from the world, as in various forms of Platonism; rather, the richness of the world is that which bears witness to the beauty of the Father in the Word. All things exist for the glory of God, and so all things must return to God.

Origen set himself the task of confronting the complexity of the world and beginning the slow process of bringing order to it. This is a result, not of chaos, but of the richness of the created world's participation in the divine *Logos*.[2] This is not to say that he wants to master the world, but simply that he wants to demonstrate the richness of God's own life exhibited in the complexities of the created order. In this sense, as Origen states in a tidy summation of his eschatology in *On First Principles*, "The end will be like the beginning" Origen understood himself as a pedagogue, as someone

2. Williams, "Origen: Between Orthodoxy and Heresy," 12.

3. Origen, *On First Principles* 1.6, trans. G. W. Butterworth (Notre Dame: Christian Classics, 2013).

training people to think deeply about the way they live in the world. Becoming attentive to complexity is not a way of escaping the world into an abstract philosophical system. Rather, it is a way of entering more fully into the complex relations that constitute our world and the complex set of texts the Christian tradition counts as canonical, which provide us with a lens through which to engage. In short, for Origen eschatology is about ordering our very lives toward their source: God.

That all things return to God, who is the beginning, brings us explicitly to the realm of eschatology. For Origen, creation and eschaton are inextricably held together. "Eschatology corresponds to 'archaeology.'" Further, it is with eschatology that we see "Origen's personal system in its most characteristic form." This system has two axes: divine providence and creaturely freedom. All that God creates is good, and sin is "the withdrawal of the will from the good. Therefore the question—the only question—is to know how free creatures are to return to the good."[4] This is to say two things at once: that the creature will return to God of its own freedom, and that God providentially guides and orders things to God's self (the Good). We must be immediately careful not to think of this as if God and the creature were two agencies competing for the same space, as if the universe were providentially manipulated in a fatally irresistible way. Instead, God is a great teacher: "It might be said that being a *didaskalos* [teacher/pedagogue] himself, Origen regarded his God as a *Didaskalos* too, as a Master in charge of the education of children, and looked on God's universe as a vast *didaskaleion* in which every single thing contributed to the education of the free human beings at school there."[5] The universe is a school of discipleship designed and ordered by God toward the education of his creatures in the Good.

Speaking this way of eschatology means that Origen talks about both a historical eschaton and a spiritual eschaton present here and now. For the end of all creatures is the life of God, which is present here and now and will also be historically realized in the future when all things are restored: "There is a twofold resurrection: the one by which we in spirit, will and faith rise with Christ from what is earthly so as to turn our minds to what is heavenly and seek out the things to come; and the other one which will be the general resurrection of all in the flesh."[6] Here echoing the writer of Colossians,

---

4. Daniélou, *Origen*, 276.
5. Daniélou, *Origen*, 276.
6. Hans Urs von Balthasar, *Origen: Spirit and Fire; A Thematic Anthology of His Writings* (Washington, DC: Catholic University of America Press, 2001), 883.

Origen sees God as the great pedagogue, the one who guides us through the world of trial, bringing about the resurrection in us.

Evil "is certainly real, but it can be conducive to good and it will eventually cease to exist. Hence the existence of evil is consistent with the goodness of God. When God created the world he knew that evil would one day come into it, because where there are creatures endowed with freedom it is inevitable."[7] Hence the significance of inner transformation for Origen. The world will be transformed by the transformation of human freedom under the guidance of divine providence. Further, this means the crucifixion of the world in the realization of the disclosure of divine beauty. As divine beauty is disclosed, the world is shown to be but a shadow of what is to come: "there is a second coming of Christ in the mature. . . . They have become accomplished lovers of his beauty. . . . For if the world is crucified to the just, this has also become for them the end of the world."[8]

Here we can see quite clearly why it is difficult to charge Origen with a straightforward Platonizing of the gospel. In this instance, those who have become lovers of the beauty of Christ are those who have come to glory in his cross. It is the crucified Lord who comes into the soul of the believer and by whom the world itself becomes crucified to the believer. So, then, this divine pedagogy is a pedagogy of the cross in which we see the same life that will burst forth in resurrection.

Origen's notion of God as the great pedagogue has been identified by some as a way of articulating his universalism.[9] The logic here is that God will guide all things toward their end eventually. We may find texts in Origen that suggest something like this. Yet there are moments when we also see something different. For instance, in his *Homilies on Genesis and Exodus* Origen states, "Do you wish to hear, however, the terrible voice of God when he is displeased? . . . [It] is the end when we are no longer reproached for sins, when we are no longer corrected. For then, when we have exceeded the measure of sinning 'the jealous God' turns his jealousy away from us."[10]

If God is the one who is guiding us by benevolent wrath toward God's self, when God removes God's hand we cease to be corrected. If we cease to be corrected by the grace of God's wrath, we are left to our sins. This is, for

7. Hamilton, *Origen*, 454.

8. Balthasar, *Origen: Spirit and Fire*, 885.

9. R. P. C. Hanson, *Allegory and Event: A Study of the Sources and Significance of Origen's Interpretation of Scripture* (Richmond: John Knox, 1959), 335.

10. Origen, *Homilies on Genesis and Exodus*, ed. Ronald E. Heine (Washington, DC: Catholic University of America Press, 1981), 328.

Origen and for much of the Christian tradition, a very real and terrifying way of speaking of the end of the reprobate. Divine indifference is the ultimate curse. As Origen states elsewhere on Romans, "So then, God bears with everyone patiently and awaits each one's repentance; but this should not render us negligent or make us slow to conversion, since there is a definite measure to his patience and forbearance."[11]

While these texts certainly do seem to be in some degree of conflict with others, we should remember that Origen was not interested in a system first and foremost. Rather, he was interested in dealing with the complexity of the world as we face it. Rather than attempting to resolve this in a straightforward system, which runs the risk of riding roughshod over all manner of perplexities, he attempted to dwell in difficulty. In sum, in Origen eschatology takes something of a turn away from the chiliasm of some of the earlier fathers—such as Irenaeus, who expected an imminent end to history—and becomes more and more about the imminent ordering of creaturely life toward its transcendent end in God. God, as the beginning of all things, is the end of all things. And yet this is emphatically not to collapse everything into a deterministic historical scheme, for both God and the free creature are always dynamically involved in the forming of creaturely agency. Eschatology is for Origen, then, a way of speaking of divine pedagogy.

Julian of Norwich (1342–1416)

We now move into the Middle Ages and a consideration of Julian of Norwich, one of the most significant figures in medieval British theology. Like many in this period, she remains something of an elusive figure. Without a formal theological education, as was usual for a woman of the period, she displayed an agile mind that showed theological affinities with many of the great figures of the western tradition.[12] Julian is known for her "shewings," the *Revelations of Divine Love*, a text detailing and reflecting upon revelations she received. Yet, we have two texts, a short text and a long text. The short text was written some twenty years prior to the long text. So we must be

11. Origen, *Commentary on the Epistle to the Romans, Books 1–5*, trans. Thomas P. Scheck, The Fathers of the Church (Washington, DC: Catholic University of America Press, 2001), 106.

12. Denys Turner notes in particular the many Augustinian and Thomistic tropes that appear throughout Julian's work. See Denys Turner, *Julian of Norwich, Theologian* (New Haven: Yale University Press, 2011), 3–31. Grace Jantzen has a helpfully concise discussion of Julian's education in her book *Julian of Norwich* (London: SPCK, 1987), 15–27.

careful not to think of Julian's "shewings" as a variety of religious experience, if by that we mean something disconnected from a life of careful thought and contemplation. Julian would not have thought about her "shewings" in this modern way. If we are to think of Julian through the existential type, it will be after the manner of Origen, for Julian was concerned with thinking through the journey of all things back to God.

Julian was an anchoress, meaning she lived a life of seclusion and contemplation, in contrast to cenobitic orders in which one would submit to communal rhythms of life. She also lived in the midst of a tumultuous period in the Middle Ages. The fourteenth century is often described by historians as a period of crisis. During her lifetime the Black Death swept Europe, reaching England mid-century, killing an estimated 30 to 60 percent of the total population. England had become embroiled in the Hundred Years' War (1337–1453), a drawn-out series of conflicts over the kingdom of France, with the civil conflict known as the Wars of the Roses to follow (1455–1487). Further, across Europe the Holy Roman Empire was in decline and the papacy in crisis. Julian was a contemporary of the Western Schism (1378–1417), a period in which multiple claimants to the papacy contested for authority. The decline of the Holy Roman Empire had begun with the earlier Interregnum (1257–1273), in which no German prince could gain universal power. Fighting internal to the empire persisted from this stage until its eventual collapse.

It is little surprise, then, that many of the themes that concern theologians and various other thinkers in this tumultuous period are those of death, sin, and suffering. While the question of theodicy is a much later question arising after Gottfried Leibniz (1646–1716), the question of how "all shall be well," in Julian's words, is front and center. This is inevitably an eschatological question insofar as it is concerned with the path of the world back to the good, to God. The question arises in Julian as it relates to the question of the relationship between sin and divine love.

Structurally, Julian's thought can be difficult to grasp; it often appears to be diffuse and rambling. However, there are themes that emerge again and again throughout her *Revelations* that bear a strikingly systematic contour. Her theology is spiraling.[13] One can move in a circular motion, returning to the same territory again and again, or one can move in a straight line, always covering the same territory. But to move in a spiral is to return to the same territory in a different way. It is this which gives Julian's theology its

13. Turner, *Julian of Norwich, Theologian*, 4.

systematic character, as she probes the question of sin and divine providence from a multiplicity of shifting vantage points.

Moving to the content of the *Revelations*, we see that in chapter 45 Julian faces a perplexity. On the one hand, she sees that "God judges us according to the essence of our human nature, which is always kept united in him, whole and safe without end; and this judgement derives from his righteousness." On the other hand, "man judges on the basis of a changeable sensory being, which seems now one thing and then another according to how it is variously influenced and appears outwardly."[14] The mixed judgment of humans is disclosed in the fact that at one moment it is good and tolerant, which "pertains to God's righteousness," and in another moment it can be severe. Christ's work is to reform our judgment and "bring it to righteousness" (*RDL*, 98, chap. 45). That is to say, God's presence in the world is in the form of a narrative of the reform of human beings, and yet this narrative requires brokenness, which creates a tension.

The eschatological import of this tension is borne out at the beginning of the next revelation. Julian states, "our fleeting life that we lead here in our sensory being does not know what our self is, except through our faith" (*RDL*, 99, chap. 46). It is only at the end, when all is made well, that we come to understand who we are. In this sense, who we are remains bound up in divine eternity, for God is the one who narrates our being. So, Julian continues, it is proper for us "both through nature and through grace, to long and desire with all our might to know ourselves, and in this full knowledge we shall clearly and truly know our God, in fullness of endless joy" (*RDL*, 99, chap. 46). Coming to know ourselves and coming to know God are intimately bound together, for we remain obscure to ourselves so long as we sinfully wrench ourselves away from God. Indeed, we remain obscure to ourselves until the eschaton. Julian details that she, paradoxically, "saw in the same revelation that many mysteries remain hidden" (*RDL*, 100, chap. 46), so we can only maintain faith and hope that both we and God will be, finally, revealed.

Divine narrative forms the ground of Julian's affirmation that all shall be well. Yet her confidence in the divine narrative is not grounded in any bland optimism that things will get better. It is grounded in mystery and uncertainty. Here we see one of the most interesting aspects of Julian's eschatology, its apophatic, or negative, character. The apophatic traditions in Christian

14. Julian of Norwich, *Revelations of Divine Love*, trans. Barry Windeatt (Oxford: Oxford University Press, 2015), 98, chap. 45. Hereafter *RDL*.

theology maintain that it is impossible to speak of God adequately, and that we must embrace a kind of learned ignorance, in the words of Nicholas of Cusa.[15] In this sense, Julian has not claimed to see the end of history, for that would be to claim to see those mysteries revealed. She has claimed that it is only as we abandon ourselves to a certain kind of ignorance, grounded in faith that God is good in spite of our sin, that we can hope that all shall be well. As she states, her hope "was in the endless love, in which I saw I should be protected by his mercy, and brought to his bliss" (RDL, 101, chap. 47). The reason this hope must be maintained is that our sight is often distracted, and we fall into blindness (RDL, 101, chap. 47).

Julian realized that the kind of ecstatic sight she had throughout her Revelations "cannot be continuous in this life," for we are frail. Yet it is not our sight which is of ultimate significance; it is God's. "Our failing is full of fear, our falling is full of shame, and our dying is full of sorrow; but throughout all this the sweet eye of pity never looks away from us, nor does the operation of mercy cease" (RDL, 102, chap. 48). The divine gaze precedes and follows us in spite of our deferred gaze. Our gaze may stray, but the constancy of the divine gaze is what allows us to "fall" and to "fail" without losing ourselves. Slowly and invisibly, then, God "works continually to bring us into an endless peace" (RDL, 104, chap. 49). For Julian, sight functions eschatologically. To see God is to be at peace, to love. Yet, to take one's eyes off God is to fall into sin. The continuous vision of God, in this life at least, is impossible. It is only eschatologically that one's sight can be restored. The constancy of the divine gaze, which is the divine love, is the ground of our hope. It is to hope that all shall be well.

Hans Urs von Balthasar (1905–1988)

From the medieval period we now enter modernity and turn our attention to the Swiss-German theologian Hans Urs von Balthasar, who was one of the most significant theological figures of the twentieth century, and whose influence continues today in a number of different streams of theological discourse. Along with a diverse array of thinkers such as Joseph Ratzinger (who would become Pope Benedict XVI), Henri de Lubac, Hans Küng, and Pierre Teilhard de Chardin, Balthasar was a part of the nouvelle théologie or

---

15. Nicholas of Cusa, On Learned Ignorance, trans. Jasper Hopkins (Minneapolis: Arthur J. Banning Press, 1985).

Ressourcement movement in mid-twentieth-century Roman Catholicism. On the fly-leaf of volume 3 of Balthasar's magnum opus, *The Glory of the Lord*, Henri de Lubac named him the "most cultured man in Europe." His encyclopaedic learning was famous and is illustrated in the sheer variety of texts he employed to craft his theology. This made him both a great treasure trove of insight and difficult to interpret at one and the same time.

Balthasar's influence on eschatological discussions in the latter half of the twentieth century and into the twenty-first can be traced to various areas of study and movements, from the nature of apocalyptic, to the emergence of Radical Orthodoxy, to the possibility of universalism.[16] His influence is most conspicuous, however, in the emergence of "drama" as a category employed to understand divine interaction with created history. As we shall see, this category places him in stark contrast with Rudolf Bultmann and his dehistoricized existential approach to eschatological questions. Balthasar's *magnum opus* is a trilogy of works exploring the classical transcendental qualities of being: truth, goodness, and beauty. His great lament was the decline of western culture into the barbarism of early twentieth-century fascism. From the outset of his career, therefore, he was interested in the relationship between the "soul" of a culture and its political and social ordering. Eventually, he came to cast the problems facing western culture in the middle of the twentieth century as playing out a much older problem in western thought: that of the division of nature from grace, philosophy from theology. This gets us to the heart of his eschatology, which, according to one commentator, is concerned with the ordering of creaturely being to communion with divine being.[17] Balthasar is concerned to diagnose the ills of modernity, and to overcome them with a theologically driven vision. In contrast to those within German liberalism and to later figures such as Bultmann, he offers little by way of compromise with modern scientific historicism.

Balthasar wrote his doctoral thesis on the subject of the "eschatological problem in modern German literature." From the outset of his career, then, he was interested in eschatological themes. However, in this early period he seemed to think that western culture had declined from the grandeur of earlier periods in Christendom. As he states in an early essay, "We are living in a time when the images of gods and idols are crashing all about us. The

16. John Milbank, Graham Ward, and Catherine Pickstock, eds., *Radical Orthodoxy: A New Theology* (London: Routledge, 1999).

17. Nicholas J. Healy, *The Eschatology of Hans Urs von Balthasar: Being as Communion* (Oxford: Oxford University Press, 2004), 210-11.

spiritual and cultural traditions of vast regions of the West are increasingly being called into question; indeed, we can go even further and say they are being liquidated, quickly and relatively painlessly."[18]

The loss of the vision of God in the present moment was bound up with the loss of analogical vision in the late Middle Ages, according to Balthasar. In order to understand how he wants to reestablish communion between God and creatures, we need to understand how he conceives of the *analogia entis*, the analogy of being. This allows us to place Balthasar in the existential type, for, like Origen and Julian, his eschatology is cast in terms of the journey of the creature back to the creator.

The analogy of being is the idea that creaturely being reflects divine being; it is analogous to divine being. Yet, because it is *analogous*, it is different from divine being. In fact, because God is infinite, creaturely being can only ever fall short of reflecting divine being adequately. So, for Balthasar, we can never identify the creature with God; and yet, because the creature is created by and for God, the creature reflects divine glory. Glory is a key concept for Balthasar, because it is through an exposition of divine glory that he begins his trilogy on aesthetics, the study of beauty. Construed theologically, the beautiful is the glorious: God's glory is God's beauty.[19] The creature participates in divine glory analogically by virtue of the communion between God and the creature established in the person of Jesus Christ, God and human. Hence, creaturely glory is a reflection of divine glory only to the extent that it is faithful to the incarnate Son of God.

Balthasar concludes the first volume of his theological aesthetics with an "Eschatological Reduction."[20] Here he brings together his vision of analogy with a vision of the end of all things. For him, the incarnation is a once-and-for-all event. This means that he does not affirm any identification of God with the creation, as a pantheist would. And, yet, like Origen, he states that the natural world itself will conform to the image of the divine Logos. The second Adam plunges into the chaos of the world and "has from the outset vanquished these forces of chaos through the freedom of his love. That which

18. Hans Urs von Balthasar, "Patristics, Scholastics and Ourselves," trans. Edward T. Oakes, *Communio* 24 (Summer 1997): 347.

19. In many ways this notion is derived from his reading of his Protestant companion, Karl Barth, who made the same claim in *Church Dogmatics* II/1, trans. Thomas F. Torrance and Geoffrey W. Bromiley (Edinburgh: T&T Clark, 1957), 608-78. This was said to be Balthasar's favorite part-volume in the *Church Dogmatics*.

20. Hans Urs von Balthasar, *The Glory of the Lord: A Theological Aesthetics*, vol. 1: *Seeing the Form*, trans. Erasmo Levia-Merikakis (San Francisco: Ignatius, 1982), 679-83.

is formless must submit to his shaping power, and rebellion itself must bend the knee with the rest of the cosmos."[21] Here Balthasar invokes images from Genesis and the New Testament together in order to locate the very end of things in their origin. God's eschatological work is God's presence in and to the creation as God remakes the world in the image of the second Adam, Jesus Christ. The presence of evil, ugliness, and disorder in the world is the presence of a creature that has dislocated itself from that which gives it form, that which sustains it in being. The end of all things is the reestablishment of the broken communion of all things with God, and so the creation will once again come to reflect divine glory, which is given us in advance in the Son of God.

In the above we have also seen Balthasar touching on a more controversial element of his eschatology, that of the relation of *all* things to God's salvific action. In his short work *Dare We Hope "That All Men Be Saved"?*, he explores the possibility of the *hope* that all things will be one day reconciled to God.[22] Marshaling resources from the Scriptures, Origen, Augustine, Thomas Aquinas, and his own theo-logic, Balthasar suggests that it is possible to hope for the reconciliation of all things with God, for inasmuch as all things come forth from God they are good. Yet this remains a hope. He is not interested in providing a watertight universalism; he simply wants to illustrate the breadth and depth of God's reconciling action, its universal significance.

Included in this discussion is also a discourse on hell. Balthasar was particularly interested in the significance for Christian theology of Holy Saturday, the day of Christ's descent into hell.[23] Holy Saturday becomes the Son of God's descent into the deepest darkness humanity will face, the darkness of hell. Since Christ has descended to these depths, no space in the cosmos remains God-forsaken. So, Balthasar notes, "when the Son passes through hell on Holy Saturday, he does so as one to whom the Father shows his secret because he no longer keeps it for himself; he is coming to know what is excluded from the light (because of God's wrath against sin as well as his love for mankind)."[24] The Father, then, takes the Son into the heart of darkness,

21. Balthasar, *The Glory of the Lord*, 1:679.

22. Hans Urs von Balthasar, *Dare We Hope "That All Men Be Saved"? With a Short Discourse on Hell*, trans. David Kipp and Lothar Krauth (San Francisco: Ignatius, 2014).

23. He discusses this in volume 5 of his *Theo-Drama*: Hans Urs von Balthasar, *Theo-Drama: Theological Dramatic Theory*, vol. 5: *The Last Act*, trans. Graham Harrison (San Francisco: Ignatius, 1998), 311–40.

24. Balthasar, *Theo-Drama*, 5:337.

into God's wrath, so that this wrath is exhausted, for the Son "will divert the scourge of eternal wrath on to himself."[25] God's judgment is, then, included in God's grace. This is the possibility of *hope* for universal salvation.

Rudolf Bultmann (1884–1976)

Karl Rahner's examination of an "existential approach" to reading eschatological assertions implicitly refers to the highly influential work in the mid-twentieth century of Rudolf Bultmann. Although Bultmann's work is also theologically important, he is best known as a giant among twentieth-century New Testament scholars (his form-critical approach came to dominate the field in Germany). The son of a German Lutheran pastor, he studied at Tübingen, Berlin, and Marburg before becoming professor of New Testament at Marburg. His work signals a revision of what is meant by eschatological language in order to radicalize the encounter of faith. However, that revision also signals a detemporalization of the eschatological. That is to say, the apocalyptic moment of God's encounter with the human is removed from the realm of historical occurrence and relocated into the moment of faith. In this sense, Bultmann's thought is also a radicalization of Lutheran apocalyptic and its concern with the crisis of the person before God.

Demythologization

In 1941 Bultmann presented what proved to be an equally influential and infamous lecture, "The New Testament and Mythology."[26] Delivered to a conference of clergy of the Confessing Church, this lecture introduced the term "demythologization." In 1942, however, a convention of pastors in Berlin denounced the essay as heretical, although Dietrich Bonhoeffer defended it as a breath of fresh air and declared the convention to be a disgrace to the Confessing Church. Moreover, while in 1953 a pronouncement of the bishops of the United Evangelical-Lutheran Church warned theologians of

---

25. Balthasar, *Theo-Drama*, 5:335.

26. Rudolf Bultmann, "The New Testament and Mythology," in *The New Testament and Mythology and Other Basic Writings*, trans. and ed. Schubert Ogden (Minneapolis: Fortress, 1984), 1–44. Hereafter *NTM*.

the danger of abandoning key themes from the New Testament, the bishops offered a formal apology to Bultmann in 1974.

The political context of Bultmann's address is clear from the parallel paper "The Question of Natural Revelation," in which Bultmann claims that God's will cannot be read off historical phenomena, and consequently German national identity is inappropriate to measure and regulate right action. Here Bultmann criticized the Nazi-supporting German Christian Church that had equated the Third Reich with God's purposeful ways for Germany and for the whole world.

Bultmann's work reflects the key influence of his Marburg teacher Wilhelm Hermann (1846–1922), for whom true religion belonged in a realm free from speculative philosophy but also free from interference by science. Consequently, science and religion address two different sets of questions, each belonging in its own sphere. In fact, the Christian's own life of faith is grounded, not in the changing opinions of scholars about the historical veracity of the text, but rather in the Gospels' witness to the communion of Jesus with God. As Bultmann himself wrote in 1941: "To believe in the cross of Christ does not mean to concern ourselves . . . with an objective event . . . but rather to make the cross of Christ our own, to undergo crucifixion with him" (*NTM*, 35). The overtures of Luther's crisis and theology of the cross are apparent (see chapter 1).

By "myth" Bultmann meant the description of transcendent forces, particularly the unobjectifiable "Wholly Other," in objective, quasi-scientific terms. "Mythology is the use of imagery to express the other-worldly in terms of this world. . . . For instance, divine transcendence is expressed as spatial distance."[27] Bultmann claimed that the New Testament was deeply infected with an outmoded first-century worldview, and this worldview was very different from the contemporary one, which, for instance, did not admit supernatural agencies into world events and looked to purely scientific explanation. Famously he declared that "we cannot use electric lights and radios and, in the event of illness, avail ourselves of modern medicine and clinical means and at the same time believe in the spirit and wonder world of the New Testament" (*NTM*, 4). However, this did not mean that Bultmann felt constrained to read the texts in light of the standards of a stable modern perspective; rather, each and every perspective and worldview needed to be challenged.

---

27. Rudolf Bultmann, *History and Eschatology: The Presence of Eternity* (New York: Harper, 1962), 11.

Bultmann stood firmly within the main lines of the Weiss-Schweitzer portrait of biblical eschatology, particularly in accepting in principle their view that Jesus proclaimed the imminent in-breaking of an apocalyptic kingdom. Jesus's message is characterized as an eschatological message, proclaimed in the historical context of "pessimistic-dualistic" Jewish expectations about the fate of the old world, which will come to an imminent end, and God's new future.[28] Jesus points to the signs of the time and proclaims that God's reign is dawning, rather than already here. At the same time, he (that is, his presence, his deeds, his message) *is* "the sign of the time." The problem with this, Bultmann claimed, is that contemporary people cannot make sense of these images and expectations. The kingdom did not interrupt the course of history, as Jesus had imagined. "Of course, Jesus was mistaken in thinking that the world was destined to come to an end."[29] The *parousia* has been delayed; it never took place in the way the New Testament expected.

Bultmann identified a number of themes that demonstrated the pervasiveness of mythology throughout the New Testament: the three-tier universe (heaven, earth, and hades) as the arena for conflict between the forces of God and Satan; the Son of God's coming from heaven and defeat of evil's forces; Christ's returning on the clouds as executor of God's final judgment; the virgin birth; the bodily resurrection; and Christ's ascension.[30] The eschatology of the Bible, especially that of the apocalyptic writings, Bultmann believed, is thoroughly mythological in form.

The delay of the *parousia* is keenly felt in the New Testament. But Bultmann interpreted the significance of Jesus's message in a quite different way from Weiss and Schweitzer. They had rediscovered the essential eschatological import of Jesus's message and had raised an important barrier to the simplistic liberal assumption of Jesus as an ethical teacher, indicating instead that Jesus was a preacher of the apocalyptic. But they did not see any present theological usefulness in Jesus's message. They were only able to see Jesus's teachings as products of their time from which, according to Schweitzer, modern humanity could legitimately glean inspiration for renouncing the values of the world and accepting the importance of love. In contrast, the demythologization program enabled Bultmann to reinstate the possibility

28. Rudolf Bultmann, *Theology of the New Testament* vol. 1, trans. Kendrick Grobel (London: SCM, 1952), 4-5.

29. Rudolf Bultmann, *Primitive Christianity in Its Contemporary Setting*, trans. R. H. Fuller (Edinburgh: Fontana, 1956), 109.

30. To these myths he added the later dogmatic theories of the incarnation, atonement, and Trinity.

of the contemporary theological usefulness of eschatological discourse. The eschatological material cannot be interpreted in terms of *Historie* (scientific history reconstructing past events) but rather must be read in terms of their *Sache* (subject matter) as *Geschichte* (history in its existential impact on contemporary life).

The demythologization program was a way of, first, "deobjectifying" these naïve theological conceptions of the biblical writers and, second, asking what they were trying to say through their mythological or objectifying conceptuality.[31] Therefore, while the term "demythologization" might suggest a stripping away of the husk in order to discover the kernel, a negative hermeneutical exercise, Bultmann had something more positive in mind. "To demythologize is to deny that the message of Scripture and of the Church is bound to an ancient world-view which is obsolete."[32] Bultmann did not wish to simply jettison the ancient thought forms, but rather intended to understand their true message, their subject matter, and to discipline one's reading in the light of that message.

Now, for Bultmann, if the biblical myths are to be interpreted, how are they to be interpreted? What is the underlying truth of the myths that can provide the key to correct interpretation? His claim is that the *kerygma* has to be interpreted in the existential and self-involving language of human existence, encounter, and decision—or more simply, "faith." In other words, the true meaning of the myths lies in their understanding of human existence. "Myth should be interpreted not cosmologically, but anthropologically, or better still, existentially."[33] Using terms coined by his earlier Marburg colleague, the philosopher Martin Heidegger, Bultmann identified two fundamental possibilities of human existence: authentic and inauthentic existence; or, in theological terms, in/under faith and without faith. In faith, human existence can realize a new possibility of forgiveness, freedom, and love that comes as a gift of God's judgment and grace through proclamation of the word of the cross. Bultmann turned particularly to writings of Paul and John for support for his existential interpretation.

31. H. P. Owen suggests that "Demythologizing would be more accurately called deobjectifying." Owen, *Revelation and Existence: A Study in the Theology of Rudolf Bultmann* (Cardiff: University of Wales Press, 1957), 15.

32. Rudolf Bultmann, *Jesus Christ and Mythology* (New York: Charles Scribner's Sons, 1958), 36.

33. Bultmann, "The New Testament and Mythology," 10.

Existential Apocalyptic

For Bultmann the crucial thing about Jesus's ministry and proclamation was that it created a crisis demanding a decision. "The future element in the proclamation is not so much temporal as existential; it is future in the sense that it is coming towards men and demanding a decision of them."[34] In Bultmann's demythologizing program, then, the kingdom is ever coming and thus ceases to be a future event that is and can be hoped for. Since the decision is a continual decision, the kingdom of God is not an event in time. Thus the kingdom, emptied of its temporal content, transcends time without ever entering it. In short, the kingdom of God is primarily understood in existentialist fashion as the hour for the individual's decision.

As Bultmann understood it, the earliest Christians were alarmed when Jesus did not return in their lifetimes. Faced with the difficult prospect of perceiving this expectation of the imminent *parousia* as meaningless and erroneous, the early church reinterpreted its founder's eschatological message. The singular character of Jesus was then understood in a new way. The early church understood "Jesus as the one whom God by the resurrection has made Messiah" and so "awaited him as the coming Son of Man."[35] Jesus's coming, cross, and resurrection had the meaning of an eschatological occurrence, and therefore the earliest church regarded itself as a community of the end of days. Since the hoped-for *parousia* did not occur, Christians eventually put off the end of the world in a more and more distant and unknown future (Heb. 1:2; 9:26; 1 Pet. 4:7; Barnabas 21:3; Ignatius, Eph. 11:1). In "Man between the Times," Bultmann explained this change in the understanding of the *parousia*, saying that this move "has been made in many circles without any discontinuity or difficulty . . . , there is no sign of impatience or disappointment."[36]

Bultmann characterized the early church as an eschatological community.[37] When the earliest church proclaimed Jesus as the coming Messiah or the Son of Man, it stayed within the frame of Jewish eschatological expectations. The earliest community understood itself to be standing "between the times," an "interim" people at the end of the old aeon and at the beginning of the new one (see 1 Cor. 15:23–27). The difference between these Chris-

34. Norman Perrin, *The Kingdom of God in the Teaching of Jesus* (London: SCM, 1963), 115.

35. Bultmann, *Theology of the New Testament*, 1:43–44.

36. Bultmann, in *Existence and Faith: Shorter Writings of Rudolf Bultmann*, ed. and trans. Schubert Ogden (London: World, 1963), 296.

37. Bultmann, *Theology of the New Testament*, 1:37–39.

tians and the Jewish apocalypticists was that the former believed that the new aeon was already breaking in and that its powers were already at work and discernable. Moreover, the Christian community had been, in a certain sense, already freed from the old aeon, instead belonging to the new one. It understood itself as the community of the last days, as the true Israel, the "elect" and "saints." As Bultmann explained, though Paul still described the eschatological judgment in apocalyptic terms as a future event, decisive is what now happens to our own existence. Hence Bultmann speaks of faith as an eschatological occurrence for Paul. Thus it is unnecessary for us today to understand the goal of history as some apocalyptic cataclysm. Even Paul's hope that the great drama of eschatological events might occur during his lifetime is labeled by Bultmann as an unimportant sideline in Paul's actual eschatological outlook. "We are confronted with the eschaton in the Now of encounter."[38]

Feminist Theologies

Throughout the nineteenth and twentieth centuries, feminism has been a potent politically and socially transformative movement. Feminisms vary greatly depending upon their particular contextual locations. Broadly speaking, however, we tend to speak of three distinct waves of feminist thought.

First-wave feminism is associated with the suffragette movements, though its origins were even earlier, with intellectual and social trailblazers such as Mary Wollstonecraft, author of *A Vindication of the Rights of Women* (1792). With the coming of World War I, many women found themselves performing social roles and work that had been traditionally seen as the domain of men. This gave impetus to suffrage movements and raised the question of women's roles and rights with a new vigor and reality.

After World War II, second-wave feminisms emerged, which are largely associated with figures such as Simon de Beauvoir and, in theology, Rosemary Radford Ruether, Catherine LaCugna, and Elizabeth Johnson. These forms of feminism have been concerned to advocate for the equality of women with men. They have been responsible for large strides in female reproductive rights, the rights of sex-workers, workplace equality, etc.

In the later part of the twentieth century, questions of homosexuality,

38. Rudolf Bultmann, *Kerygma and Myth: A Theological Debate*, vol. 1 (London: SPCK, 1956), 116.

gender, and systemic justice came to mingle in many ways, and feminists began to join cause with others, such as queer theorists. Third-wave feminisms, then, have come to disrupt many of the categories in which gender itself is constructed, with implications for other issues surrounding human sexuality and sociality. These feminisms have contested the ways femininity, masculinity, and heterosexuality are themselves culturally constructed. While earlier feminisms had focused upon recovering the rights of a particular gender, these feminisms were questioning the very way gender was construed in the first place. Why, for instance, were women historically cast as homemakers? Was this something *essentially* feminine, established in a fixed order of things, or was this something *culturally* constructed and therefore potentially more fluid? Key here is the work of Judith Butler, Grace Jantzen, Sarah Coakley, and Catherine Keller, among others.

Feminism is another example of a pressure being placed upon God-talk and talk of the end of all things. In this case, it is the realization that much God-talk has historically assumed a sexist guise; and, potentially, the way in which the end has been spoken of has been shrouded in this sexist language. For example, many of the images within apocalyptic literature are violent, and often women appear in an unsavory light. We shall see that how we speak about God and particularly God's power comes to shape how we speak of the end of all things as well as our contemporary situation.

The eschatological significance of feminist movements is located in this chapter because feminism is concerned with changing a social order from within, and so is concerned with questions surrounding the end of human sexuality and gender as well as the importance of women's experience to the task of theology. Questions emerge such as: What is gender for? Does it have any final significance for how we speak of God? But, more than this, feminism has provided the theological world with a variety of new perspectives on all manner of traditional Christian doctrinal categories because it has provided women with a voice often previously muffled. Much of feminist discourse is about interrupting and pointing out many of the gendered assumptions of traditional doctrine, as well as shedding new light on the same material. Two examples of this are Catherine Keller and Sarah Coakley.

Catherine Keller

Catherine Keller's work stands at the intersection of a number of theological discourses. Here it is crucial to note that she is interested in appropriating

46

feminist thought within a process ontology. Process thought posits that God is bound by a movement through history and so "emerges" with the creation through time. God, then, can change, contingent upon the decisions and actions of God's creatures.[39] Keller often deploys resources from literary criticism, biblical studies, philosophy, and history in a complex patchwork. She does so, broadly speaking, in order to construct her theological musings from the ground upward. In this sense, of the two thinkers engaged here, she is the one who most neatly fits the type of an eschatology "from below."

In *Apocalypse Now and Then: A Feminist Guide to the End of the World*, Keller tackles contemporary, medieval, and ancient apocalypticisms in order to construct what she calls a "counter-apocalyptic" imagination.[40] She wants to avoid both apocalypticism and anti-apocalypticism, for she sees both of these as problematic forms of historical closure. On the one hand, should we embrace futurist apocalyptic forms of thought wholeheartedly (see chapter 1), we run the risk of mapping history neatly and removing any sense of the historical dynamism Keller wants to maintain within her process system. For process thought, the openness of God to human decision, to possibility, is critical to the structure of history itself. On the other hand, then, should we offer a form of anti-apocalyptic, an outright rejection of apocalyptic thought, Keller thinks we risk performing a corresponding form of closure, the denial of the apocalyptic. She deliberately structures her work in defiance of both forms of closure, continually making reference to the "spiral" character of her text, and enjoining the reader to potentially jump in at any point. That is to say, her work continually covers similar territory in different ways, attempting to be sensitive to the multitude of voices she is engaging (*ANT*, 12).

Positively, Keller wants to offer a counter-apocalyptic. Here gendered conversations emerge explicitly. Deploying the language of Revelation, she states, "We may yet outlast the opposition of an 'essentialist' feminist identity, which tends to reify sex, versus an 'anti-essentialist' feminist cultural constructivism that tends to disembody sex. . . . [T]he pneumatic play of spirit

---

39. Process thought originated with Alfred North Whitehead's book *Process and Reality* (corrected edition, ed. David Ray Griffin and Donald W. Sherburne [New York: Free Press, 1978]). It has important antecedents in Enlightenment and early modern (seventeenth- to nineteenth-century) pantheisms, such as those propounded by Baruch Spinoza, Gottfried Leibniz, and G. W. F. Hegel. See David Ray Griffin, "Process Eschatology," in *The Oxford Handbook to Eschatology*, ed. Jerry L. Walls (Oxford: Oxford University Press, 2010).

40. Catherine Keller, *Apocalypse Now and Then: A Feminist Guide to the End of the World* (Minneapolis: Fortress, 2009). Hereafter *ANT*.

at the boundaries of the sexual binary opens options for what is biblically speaking both male and female and neither male nor female" (*ANT*, 275).

Keller plays with several ideas here. First, she identifies the gendered character of apocalyptic language: "virgin mothers" and "prophet whores." She wants to contest these identities, but she also wants to be careful about identifying an "essentialized" female identity. That is to say, she intends to avoid constraining female identity over and against male identity in much the same way as second-wave feminists have been criticized by third-wave feminists. Yet, second, she also hopes to avoid deconstructing sexual differences in such a way that the very concrete embodied differences between the sexes cease to be meaningful. This is what she means by a "feminist cultural constructivism." Finally, positively, she wants to play at the boundaries of sexual identities, neither conflating nor separating male and female.

Keller's use of process thought ascribes eschatological significance to the evolutionary character of reality. God and the world are in a process of evolutionary interdependence and emergence. She hopes to generate a "'third' space, open but not empty, in which the presuppositions of endism may be positively overcome—'sublated,' at once preserved and transcended. . . . A way never known in advance. . . . A way that appears only as we walk there" (*ANT*, 275-76). The use of "third" here is quite deliberately an echo of the language of the "third wave" and its insistence on the fluidity of gender. Keller wants to see this fluidity as something that is continually historically emerging. This is consistent with process thought. In that sense she wants to propose a merging of eschatology and pneumatology, because it is the Spirit in whom the world is continually moving and changing (*ANT*, 275). What we hope for is continually shifting as human possibilities are enacted and opened, as history develops, in spite of apocalyptic attempts to end history.[41] Crucial for Keller is that this is a noncoercive movement that always allows for freedom and change. Hence hope is continually shifting as differing possibilities for the future emerge.

Keller's eschatology is complex, for it requires the divesting of any notion of eschatology as a movement toward a fixed end point in history. The end is continually changing as creation is reshaped by God's creative emergence with the world. Hence gendered identity is in eschatological flux. There can be no final pinning down of "femininity" or "masculinity," because these are continually being displaced and replaced.

41. Whitehead, *Process and Reality*, 12.

Sarah Coakley

Sarah Coakley's work is similar to Keller's in several substantial ways. Both operate in the wake of the significant work of third-wave feminists, both are concerned to displace gendered identity eschatologically, and both are concerned with the significance of premature eschatological closure. Yet, Coakley's work differs significantly from Keller's because she is not a process thinker and therefore does not place God in the same historical scheme. Coakley remains significantly indebted to older theological thought within the Christian and Neoplatonic traditions.

In "*Kenōsis* and Subversion: On the Repression of Vulnerability in Christian Feminist Writing," Coakley is concerned to rehabilitate the Pauline (Phil. 2:5) notion of *kenōsis* (self-emptying) for feminist thought.[42] As she shows, resistance to *kenōsis* among many feminist theologians is strong. For instance, Daphne Hampson states categorically that "for women, the theme of self-emptying and self-abnegation is far from helpful as a paradigm."[43] Coakley, in contrast, sees *kenōsis* as a crucial category for undoing patriarchal violence, because of its universal applicability to all human persons, male and female. *Kenōsis* challenges notions of masculinity and femininity that are adversarial, grounded in the assertion of power of one over and against the other. *Kenōsis* becomes, for Coakley, a spiritual practice of laying oneself bare before God and others, refusing to wield power over and against the other. So, as she states in a later work, the task of the feminist theologian is to "do the kneeling work that ultimately slays patriarchy at its root."[44] This theological undoing of gendered hierarchy in imitation of Christ lies at the root of Coakley's feminism.

Coakley's work on *kenōsis* can be traced through much of her writing from the mid-1990s onward, and its most mature form is to be found in the first volume of her systematic theology, *God, Sexuality, and the Self.* Here we see the explicitly eschatological character of her work emerge. Her central preoccupation is to embed the practice of theology in the spiritual practices of contemplation and dispossession, that is, in the deliberate refusal to use coercive power over both others and oneself in careful and attentive

---

42. Sarah Coakley, "*Kenōsis* and Subversion: On the Repression of Vulnerability in Christian Feminist Writing," in *Powers and Submissions: Spirituality, Philosophy, Gender* (Oxford: Blackwell, 2002), 3–39.

43. Daphne Hampson, *Theology and Feminism* (Oxford: Basil Blackwell, 1990), 155.

44. Sarah Coakley, *God, Sexuality, and the Self: An Essay "On the Trinity"* (Cambridge: Cambridge University Press, 2014), 327.

practices of silence before God. Coercive forms of power emerge as *desires* to dominate and lord over God, self, and others. By embedding theology within the practice of prayer and contemplation, Coakley pays particularly close attention to the ways in which theology is ordered toward an end— God. This end is bound up with divine and human desire. God is at one and the same time the object of our desire and our desire itself. As we learn to pray, we learn to desire God, and our desire is inflamed further and further as we are drawn, allured, into the divine life itself. As she summarizes her project, "From sexuality and the self to participation in the trinitarian God: this way lies a long haul of erotic purgation, but its goal is one of infinite delight."[45] When compared with Origen, Julian, and Balthasar, Coakley's form of eschatology resembles these more classical forms of our existential type much more than the more modern theologies of Bultmann and process thinkers such as Keller.

45. Coakley, *God, Sexuality, and the Self*, 11.

3. Political

It is commonly assumed that eschatology has to do with *eschata*, last things. This assumption is reflected in the number of books bearing just such a title, as well as books that are devoted to one or more of the supposed last things: resurrection, the intermediate state, the last judgment, heaven and hell. The Lutheran theologian Abraham Colovius (1612–1686) of Wittenberg coined the term "eschatology" precisely in order to frame a discussion of the final or ultimate things of God beyond the consummation of the history of the world.

Among many criticisms that have been offered of this commonly advocated approach is that it relegates eschatology and the hope that it generates and sustains to the end of a dogmatic system, remote from other matters of theology and Christian practice. A quite different set of approaches asks how hope contributes to the embodiment of a faithful witness in the world—the *politics of hope*. This set of political questions is not to be understood as something added on to Christian hope's proper business, as if it is but one element of hope. Rather, it is the requisite effect or embodiment of, or living in, hope. Hope *is* political; it witnesses to a way of life, to being made disciples together by the love of God. While this perspective featured frequently among twentieth-century theologians, the rich connections with theological themes and with the faithful life have a considerably longer theological history. Post-apostolic Christian communities (the communities following the time of the apostles), for instance, were not characterized by the kind of hope that pushes the impact of the anticipated presence of God's consummating work into some remote future, far from the effects of the presence of God in everyday life.

The Scriptures

The biblical materials offer a diverse set of conceptual emphases, emerging from communities with a plurality of interests and concerns. Nonetheless, there are several noticeable overlaps and common themes. According to the patristic scholar J. N. D. Kelly, "in the apostolic age, as the New Testament documents reveal, the Church was pervaded with an intense conviction that the hope to which Israel looked forward yearningly had at last been fulfilled. In the coming of Christ, and in His death and resurrection, God had acted decisively, visiting and redeeming His people."[1] The "delay" of the *parousia* or consummating presence of Christ is explicitly referred to in 2 Peter 3:1-10 and 1 Thessalonians 4:13-18 (see also John 21:22-23; Acts 1:6), and interpreting, managing, and redirecting these expectations among early Christian communities is one of the activities in which several New Testament writers engage.

Crucially, there appears to be little significant theological angst among these authors when the earliest generation of followers of Jesus passed its witness on to another generation, and to another after that. In succeeding periods of Christian writing, any tension between the divine eschatological promise and its fulfillment, the already and the not-yet, was cast in ways that increasingly picked up on apostolic themes concerning the redemptive re-ordering of life in the world. Accordingly, later traditions sought to navigate their way through, and to make some sense of, this eschatological tension by refusing to live in the world in despair or in a kind of longing for God's consummating presence that would evade the healing of the conditions of life in the here and now.

The Politics of Hope and the Hebrew Bible

Hope in the redemptive purposes of God remains an important motif in the Jewish Scriptures. But the form of that hope shifts from one stage to another: offspring and the land for Abraham in God's ancestral promises (Gen. 12:1-3; 15:18-21); the liberation and homecoming of the children of Israel for Moses; Judah's return from exile and restoration as the people of God (Isa. 49:6); the coming of justice to Israel and the whole world (Isa. 11:1-9); peaceful coexistence for all things (Ps. 98:3); the emergence of an idealized monarch

---

1. J. N. D. Kelly, *Early Christian Doctrines*, 5th ed. (London: A&C Black, 1977), 459.

(Isa. 11:1-2); the vindication of the righteous with the coming of God's kingdom (Dan. 12:2-3); and the renewal of all things (Isa. 65:17). Hope is firmly embedded in the historic communities' calling to live out their covenanted lives as the people of God, and it is crucial for the conditions that would realize the flourishing of that people together in God's freedom and just rule.

God's promises that remain unfulfilled contribute to the hope for the coming establishment of God's righteous rule. This is an eschatologically significant image in that the final form of God's purposeful rule—which embraces the entirety of the social, economic, and cultural life of the community—is always *coming to be* realized, particularly in the hopes during the period of the divided Hebrew kingdoms of Israel and Judah. In fact, several enthronement psalms celebrate that the kingship of God sustains not only the life of Israel but also that of the natural world and the other nations of the earth (Pss. 47:2; 96:10; 98:9).

The rhetoric of divine kingship has two functions in the thought of Israel.[2] Negatively, it destabilizes any regime that claims an absolute authority. It always stands over against the values and behavior of the people as well as the surrounding nations, not only as the source of their lives and flourishing, but also as their critical measure and judgment. In the paradigmatic narrative of God's confrontation with Pharaoh, the absolute imperial might of Pharaoh, seemingly beyond challenge, is delegitimated and finally overthrown through a series of contests. What tends to run through the image when appealed to in this way is Israel's concern with God's ways of making, sustaining, and renewing the people of Israel, whose fate was always precarious given the geopolitical turmoil of the surrounding regions. Often the psalms express hope that God would liberate Israel and destroy her enemies (Pss. 2; 20; 21; 72; 110). Even the performance of the Hebrew monarchs themselves is commonly one of abuse of position (e.g., Saul, David, and Solomon), and this is yet another reason why "there is throughout the scriptures an ambivalence towards monarchy"—in addition to the reason that Israel should have needed no sovereign but God.[3]

Yet, positively, God's rule offers compassion, healing, and deliverance of justice. "The Lord upholds all who are falling, and raises up all who are bowed down" (Ps. 145:14). Psalm 68 suggests that "God's reign is not simply

---

2. Walter Brueggemann, *Theology of the Old Testament: Testimony, Dispute, Advocacy* (Minneapolis: Fortress, 1997), 238-40.

3. Christopher Rowland, "Scriptures: New Testament," in *The Blackwell Companion to Political Theology*, ed. Peter Scott and William T. Cavanaugh (Malden: Blackwell, 2004), 27.

about power. It is about a relationship of caring fidelity, wherein God is in solidarity with the most vulnerable and the most needy in society."[4]

The Scriptures portray the covenant people's faithlessness to God in a series of prophetic cycles, starting with a curse or pronouncement of doom and ending with a promise of renewal and restoration. Much of the prophetic literature in particular is driven by a sense of calling, a pronouncement of impending or realized exile, and a declaration of promised homecoming. The prophets offer a radical protest against the behavior of the Hebrew people, especially with regard to their accommodation to the idolatrous practices of their neighbors and the unjust practices that contradict their responsibility for the flourishing of their own people. The prophet Amos, for example, has to dramatically reverse his people's expectations by warning that the Day of the Lord shall bring, not the light of God's deliverance of the people from their troubles and the punishment of their enemies, but the dark judgment of Israel itself (Amos 5:18-20; 9:8; Isa. 2:6-18; Joel 2:1-2; Mic. 2:1-4; Zeph. 2).

Following the turbulence, "total calamity," and "severe spiritual crisis" that came with the exile to Babylon in 587 BCE,[5] the lives of God's people were no longer shaped by king, temple, and city. In some passages, this is construed as a sentence on the corruption of the monarchy (Ezek. 34). While hopes for a return from exile abound (Ezek. 36:8-15; 37:15-23, 40-48; Isa. 40:1-5; 43:1-7, 14-21; 45:20-23), the eventual reality of restoration itself fails to live up to expectations. Consequently, in certain postexilic writings there develops an apocalyptic resetting of the prophetic woe and blessing cycle, now dramatized by a coming conflict and a vindication of the people that will finally come with the divine victory (Isa. 60:1-22; 61:1-7; 66:12-16).

The prophetic writings continue to emphasize the earlier nationalistic association of the people with the royal rule of God, in order to preserve the heritage and traditions (Neh. 13:23-31; Ezra 9-10; see also Num. 24), and some also begin to express a desire for "revenge" against the heathen nations. But in many postexilic texts, hope is extended from the restoration of Israel to the renewal of all things (Isa. 63; Ezek. 38; Hag. 2:21-22; Zech. 12:2-3).[6] Occasionally this works itself out in terms of the peace and just rule of God over all things (e.g., Isa. 65:17) in an Eden-like state of flourishing (Isa. 11:6-9).

Moreover, a strand of hope emerges, imagining that the coming fulfill-

---

4. Walter Brueggemann, *Mandate to Difference: An Invitation to the Contemporary Church* (Louisville: Westminster John Knox, 2007), 3. See Ps. 145:14-17; Deut. 10:14-18.

5. John Bright, *The Kingdom of God* (Nashville: Abingdon, 1953), 130.

6. Walther Eichrodt, *Theology of the Old Testament*, vol. 1, trans. John Baker (London: SCM, 1961), 468.

ment would be realized beyond death (e.g., Dan. 12:2). Perhaps as a result of the significant hardship and constant political insecurity endured by the postexilic Jewish communities, by the time of Second Temple Judaism the belief of some in "the resurrection of the dead" had to do with "the life of the age to come."[7] This image of a future life is juxtaposed with the image of Sheol, the shadowy state of death (Ps. 89:48), from which many will be awakened to "everlasting life" and others to "shame and everlasting contempt" (Dan. 12:2) at the end of days.

Finally, in later writings greater significance is given to hope for an idealized monarch associated with the Davidic ruler, who will realize God's victory and just rule among God's people (Isa. 11; Jer. 23:5-7; Amos 9:11-15). The root of Jesse becomes a signal to the peoples of a new era (Isa. 11:10), commanding peace to the nations (Zech. 9). In the apocalyptic tradition, following Daniel 7, there is mention of one who is preexistent and has the power to judge kings and the enemies of God, and who would vindicate the righteous (1 Enoch 46:1-6; 48:2-6; 62:5-7; 4 Ezra 12:32).

Jesus and the Kingdom of God

The phrase *basileia tou theou* (kingdom of God) is seldom used in the Fourth Gospel (John 3:3) or echoed by Paul (Rom. 14:17; 1 Cor. 6:9; 15:24), but it is central to Jesus's message in the Synoptic Gospels.[8] The first words the Gospel of Mark places on Jesus's lips are "The time is fulfilled, and the kingdom of God has come near; repent, and believe in the good news" (Mark 1:15). *Basileia* arguably means the activity of kingly ruling more than a geographically specific "kingdom" or territory.[9] Yet, this kingdom is not some otherworldly reality; it is here, in this reality, that God's rule becomes manifest, as evidenced in the Lord's Prayer: "Your kingdom come. Your will be done, on earth as it is in heaven" (Matt. 6:10).

The precedents for the idea of a this-worldly kingdom lie both in the Hebrew Bible and in the intertestamental and rabbinic literature, particularly

7. Christopher Rowland, "The Eschatology of the New Testament Church," in *The Oxford Handbook of Eschatology*, ed. Jerry L. Walls (Oxford: Oxford University Press, 2008), 57.

8. The Gospel of Matthew substitutes the term "heaven" for "God," most likely in order to avoid use of the name "God," as was Jewish convention at the time. However, 12:28 and 19:24 use the phrase "kingdom of God."

9. Gustaf Dalman, *The Words of Jesus Considered in the Light of Post-Biblical Jewish Writings and the Aramaic Language* (Edinburgh: T&T Clark, 1902).

in the significant image of God as Israel's king, whose rule is to be imaged in the rule of the kings of Israel (2 Chron. 9:8; Ps. 24:3-4; Isa. 33:13-16), whose sovereignty is over all (Pss. 22:28; 103:19; Wis. 6:4; 10:10), and who establishes God's glorious and righteous rule (Ps. 145:11-13). This imagery reveals the emergence of "a fundamental datum of Jewish eschatology that God would bring about an age of perfection in this world, when the dominance of foreign powers would be overthrown and God's righteousness revealed."[10]

The Scriptures give little information about the shape and character of the kingdom itself. The few things we do know come from Jesus's use of similes and metaphors, especially in the context of his teaching through parables.

First, Jesus modifies the expectations of his hearers by claiming that the eschatological rule of God has already drawn near (Matt. 1:15),[11] and its power is already manifest in Jesus's deeds of victory over the realm of evil (Matt. 12:28-29); thus God's rule is already present (Luke 17:20-21). Only the coming of Christ himself is unmistakably the *End* (Matt. 24:27-30), since he himself is the representative of God's eschatological presence. He is the heavenly judge or Son of Man (Dan. 7:13),[12] the eschatological prophet (Isa. 61; Luke 4:18-21), and even, although this is not wholly clear, the Davidic king in a way his contemporaries did not expect. In Luke's account, the coming of the Son of Man is the beginning of the process of liberation (Luke 21:27-28).

Second, and in consequence, Jesus's demand for an urgent response from his hearers means a *response to him* in the present (Matt. 10:32-33). The parables focus on what Jesus's hearers need to do and on the shape of lives that appropriately embody God's rule (e.g., Matt. 7:21; 19:23-30), as well as on the threatened judgment for those who refuse to respond repentantly and live faithfully (Matt. 8:1; 11:21-24; 22:1-14; Luke 10:13-15; 13:28-30; 14:16-24). This is why the Beatitudes both begin and end with a reference to the kingdom, thereby framing the message of all the others (Matt. 5:3, 10). There is little description of eternal perdition in the Synoptic Gospels beyond imagery of fiery anguish (e.g., Matt. 13:50). The notion of everlasting punishment is used to warn Jesus's listeners about the danger of not repenting, and it is therefore a device to encourage their embrace of God's just rule (e.g., Matt. 10:28).

---

10. Christopher Rowland, *Christian Origins: The Setting and Character of the Most Important Messianic Sect of Judaism* (London: SPCK, 2002), 132.

11. This text seems to refer less to the temporal imminence of the kingdom than to its presence. The Greek *ēngiken* has the sense of "has arrived."

12. There is scholarly dispute over whether Jesus was referring to himself as the eschatological Son of Man in Mark 14:62/Matt. 26:64/Luke 22:69. Rev. 1:7 makes the equation between Jesus and the Danielic coming Son of Man.

Third, Jesus's deeds, and therefore the pattern of the new life of the kingdom, were preeminently exemplified by his work of compassionate healing, inclusion of the disadvantaged, and so on. The image of the messianic banquet, for instance, indicates that God's is a *hospitable* rule (Matt. 26:29; Mark 14:25; Luke 22:18, reflecting Isa. 25:6-8). Luke 14:7-14 suggests, for instance, that all who are invited to dine at the banquet are given equal status. Moreover, the promised blessings of the poor, the hungry, and the oppressed in the Beatitudes, that their position will be reversed in the future when the kingdom of God comes (Matt. 5:3-12; Luke 6:20-23), demonstrates that God's rule transforms social and political arrangements so as to overturn many of the prevailing assumptions about status and power in Greco-Roman society. In other words, "Early Christians looked forward to the reordering of the world and its institutions."[13] And this reordering began with the assembly of God's people, whose lives were to reflect the shape of the hope they had in Christ.

Fourth, even if the signs of the kingdom's coming appear insignificant now, God's reign will be revealed in its glory. While the kingdom has *not yet* come in its fullness, it will do so. There is little evidence apart from Mark 9:1 of Jesus teaching an impending end of the world except in order to reinforce the urgency of an immediate decision for or against God. For example, by the parable of the fig tree Jesus directs "his disciples' minds, not towards the horrors of the end of the age, but towards the signs of the time of salvation."[14] What is certainly clear is that Mark's Jesus is less interested in satisfying curiosity concerning the end than in offering warnings about failing to hear Jesus's message regarding the kingdom of God and living in the shadow of its coming. The signs of the times referred to here seem to relate to the fall of Jerusalem, an event that occurred in 70 CE, and they depict general characteristics of an age not yet redeemed: false teachers (Matt. 24:4-5); wars (Matt. 24:6-7); natural disasters (Matt. 24:7); persecution of the church (Matt. 24:9-10); and the global witness to the gospel (Matt. 24:14). Even the expectation of the appearance of the Antichrist and a period of intense tribulation cannot make the end any more knowable than this (Matt. 24:21-22; Rev. 3:10; 7:14). Accordingly, the image of the Antichrist appears to represent opposition to God's rule *throughout history*.

13. Rowland, "The Eschatology of the New Testament Church," 57.
14. Joachim Jeremias, *Rediscovering the Parables*, rev. ed., trans. S. H. Hooke (London: SCM, 1966), 93. See Matt. 24:32-33/Mark 13:28-29/Luke 21:28-31.

The Resurrection of the Dead

The Old Testament portrays the dead as existing in Sheol.[15] This is the grave or a shadowy underworld, a land of darkness (Job 10:21-22) and silence (Ps. 115:17), in which God is not remembered (Pss. 6:5; 30:9; 88:11; Isa. 38:18). Here the dead are cut off from God, their source of life (Ps. 88:5). Only occasionally is there a hint of real life beyond death in the presence of God (Pss. 16:10-11; 49:15; 73:24). Possibly the examples of Enoch and Elijah are instructive here (Gen. 5:24; 2 Kings 2:11). It is not clear that Isaiah 25:8 and 26:19 and Daniel 12:2 necessarily offer belief in the resurrection of the dead, although the latter's notion of the awakening of those who "sleep" (a euphemism for death) to either life or shame is significant for the development of later traditions of eternal life/hell. This belief seems to have appeared in the Jewish literature of the intertestamental period, and it certainly flourished in the New Testament as a consequence of the confession that God raised Jesus to new life. While God's raising of Jesus is understood in various ways, it is always in terms of a *bodily* raising. It is a body that leaves the tomb empty, that can be touched by the disciples, and that can consume food.

Several features of the resurrection's theological importance need to be unpacked here. First, it is *revelatory* of God's blessing in that it is the vindication of Jesus's life and message and therefore a confirmation of his announcing of the kingdom. Second, it is itself *the eschatological event*, God's new creation and the destiny of the new human being (e.g., Rom. 6:4; 1 Cor. 15:15, 17-18, 21-22; 1 Thess. 4:14). Resurrection increasingly had come to belong to the ancient Jewish expectation of the final destiny of God's people, and so the raising of this one man declares that in him the end has begun, and therefore in him and by him others are raised and have their hope. So the raised Jesus is the "first fruits" of the general raising of the dead (1 Cor. 15:20); he has inaugurated the way that others may follow in him (1 Cor. 15:45); he is the "last Adam," the eschatological Man (1 Cor. 15:45); he is the resurrection and the life, belief in whom determines one's own being raised to life (John 11:25); and he is the one we will be like (Phil. 3:21; 1 John 3:2). That is why there is a marked difference in type between the raising of Jesus into eschatological life and the "resuscitation" of others being brought *back* from the dead to the same life (for instance, Lazarus). It is this that makes

---

15. Hades is the New Testament equivalent (Matt. 11:23; 16:18; Luke 10:15; Acts 2:27, 31; Rev. 1:18; 6:8; 20:13-14), referring usually to death or the power of death. In Luke 16:23 it is the place of torment for the wicked after death.

sense of the oddity of Jesus's post-resurrection body, which, for instance, can walk through walls (John 20:19) and disappear (Luke 24:31). Therefore, the bodies of those resurrected in Christ will be characterized by glory and incorruption (1 Cor. 15:42–44) and by having spiritual bodies (1 Cor. 15:44) wholly vitalized and transformed by the Spirit of the raised Christ. Third, as bodily resurrection, the event reaffirms God's *faithfulness* to the creation that God has blessed. Fourth, by being raised in Christ, the Christian communities are called into *new* life. Citizenship in God's kingdom is through the one raised, ascended, and made present in the Spirit. In this rule of God, the earth will be renewed and transformed, the nations will bow before God, and a time of healing and peacefulness will begin. To suggest that 1 Corinthians 15 makes the resurrection of the person part of the general resurrection presses the text too far by requiring a concept of an intermediate state, an existence *between* resurrection and consummation.

The concept of resurrection raises the question of how to interpret the idea of immortality in the New Testament, since Jesus's *being raised* (from passivity, from death) cannot allow the deadliness of death to be denied. After all, he continues to bear the scars of execution (Rev. 5:6). Humanity has descended from the fallen Adam (Rom. 5:12), which is why death is portrayed as a consequence of sin, an evil that terrorizes, an enemy of God and humanity (1 Cor. 15:26). However, Christ has destroyed death and "brought life and immortality to light" (2 Tim. 1:10). Immortality, which properly belongs to God alone (1 Tim. 6:16), is now bestowed on the faithful (Rom. 2:7) so that mortality can be clothed with immortality (1 Cor. 15:53–54).

The New Heavens and the New Earth

With the universal disclosure of God's rule in Christ, God's enemies (sin and death) will be destroyed, and God's redemptive purposes will be fulfilled. Those purposes are cosmic in scope in that they redeem all that God has created. Therefore the whole of creation will be liberated from its bondage to the suffering brought by sin (Rom. 8:19–23). The image that depicts this is that of the "new heavens and a new earth, where righteousness is at home" (2 Pet. 3:13; see also Rev. 21:1). The implication here is that Christian hope is not for redemption *from* the world (as if it is hope for a disembodied place called "heaven") but for the redemption *of* the world (Isa. 65:17; 66:22; Matt. 19:28).

Moreover, the images of the eschatological perfecting of fellowship with God (cf. Rev. 21:3, 7), the consummated worship of God (Rev. 7:15; 22:3), and

seeing God face to face (Matt. 5:8; Rev. 22:4) do not refer to the contemplation of God by *individuals*. The New Testament frequently uses corporate
images to depict the life of the redeemed with God: for instance, the eschatological banquet (Matt. 8:11; Mark 14:25; Luke 14:15–24; 22:30) or wedding
feast (Matt. 25:10; Rev. 19:9); paradise (Matt. 8:11; Mark 14:25; Luke 14:15–24;
22:30); and the heavenly Jerusalem (Heb. 12:22; Rev. 21).

Augustine (354–430)

The prolific Aurelius Augustinus, bishop of Hippo, is arguably the person
"most influential in shaping Western Christianity's understanding of traditional hopes and forebodings about the end of human life and human
history."[16] His eschatology is nonetheless often misconceived. In particular,
he is supposed to have offered a strict contrast between time and eternity,
between human existence *now* in history and the consummated life *then* in
eternity.[17] Augustine is seen as being pessimistic "about the earthly city" and
as offering "a pretty negative contribution to the topic of this-worldly hope."[18]
At the same time, it is often assumed that he equated the church with the
millennial rule of God.[19] Following from this, his *Confessions* is interpreted
as having laid the groundwork for a form of interiorization of the knowledge
of God; if so, this would suggest that it would have been better to treat him
in chapter 2 rather than at this point in our reflections.[20]

Nonetheless, this psychological reading of *Confessions* needs to be at
least somewhat tempered by several features of the book. First, written in
the form of a prayer, it makes very clear that human life is a *gift* from another, lived in response to that other.[21] Second, that the text is full of biblical

16. Brian E. Daley, "Eschatology in the Early Fathers," in Walls, *The Oxford Handbook of Eschatology*, 100.

17. Daley, "Eschatology in the Early Fathers," 100; Brian E. Daley, *The Hope of the Early Church: A Handbook of Patristic Eschatology* (Cambridge: Cambridge University Press, 1991), 132.

18. Brian Hebblethwaite, *The Christian Hope* (Basingstoke: Marshall, Morgan & Scott, 1984), 58, 56.

19. Daley, *The Hope of the Early Church*, 134; Hebblethwaite, *The Christian Hope*, 55.

20. Charles Taylor, *Sources of the Self: The Making of the Modern Identity* (Cambridge, MA: Harvard University Press, 1989), ch. 7; Phillip Cary, *Augustine's Invention of the Inner Self: The Legacy of a Christian Platonist* (Oxford: Oxford University Press, 2000).

21. Janet Soskice, "Augustine on Knowing God and Knowing the Self," in *Faithful Reading: New Essays in Theology in Honour of Fergus Kerr, OP*, ed. Simon Oliver, Karen Kilby, and Thomas O'Loughlin (London: T&T Clark, 2012), 61–74.

reflections and quotations indicates that Christians learn from, and have an ongoing dependency upon, the Christian community. Third, the goal of the soul's search is the love of God, which is deeply connected with the love of the neighbor, or the creatures of God. In fact, the privacy of the inner world is unnatural, born of sin or the distortion of desire and the will. In Augustine's account, we were not created to be alone in our private worlds but to enjoy God together. Fourth, and finally, "Augustine's distinctiveness is the refusal to present a narrative that in any sense claims clarity or finality."[22]

Augustine contested both the prevalent millenarianism, which saw the current Christianizing conditions of the Roman Empire as offering a sign that the rule of God in Christ had begun, and the apocalyptically futurist and anti-material versions of the good life.

The Constantinianizing of Hope

Before we proceed to discuss Augustine's work, the seismic shifts in the fate of the church and its relation to the empire in the early third century need to be explained. Hippolytus's *Of Christ and Antichrist* had described Rome apocalyptically as the "new Babylon." And yet, Tertullian had spoken of the emperors and the stability of the very empire itself as a "restraining force" against the impending end of all things under demonic auspices, and he called for Christians to pray for the empire's well-being (*Apology* 32). Even so, the overwhelming sense from Tertullian's work is that Christians are aliens in an inhospitable world, an understandable emphasis during a period of persecution and the witness of Christian martyrs.

During Constantine the Great's reign, however, "more change took place in the status, structure, and beliefs of the Christian Church than during any previous period of its history."[23] Arguably, this was a period in which the very sense of the eschatological imagination fundamentally changed. The ground was prepared by Lactantius, who argued that the persecutions of his day under Emperor Diocletian were the sign of a sick and crumbling world into which would arrive, at the six thousandth year of created existence, greater tribulation, political instability, and eventually the age of the victori-

---

22. Rowan Williams, *On Augustine* (London: Bloomsbury, 2016), 3.

23. T. A. Drake, "The Impact of Constantine on Christianity," in *The Cambridge Companion to the Age of Constantine*, ed. Noel Lenski (Cambridge: Cambridge University Press, 2005), 111.

ous Christ's peace for God's people. Around 314, two years after Constantine's Christian vision and his conversion to Christianity, Lactantius claimed that the emperor's "first care" was "to restore the Christians to the exercise of their worship and to their God" (*On the Deaths of the Persecutors* 24). Eusebius of Caesarea (c. 260–c. 340) wrote of something considerably more than the particular divine favor granted to one of God's own, God as "friend, protector and guardian of Constantine"; instead, there was a fundamental change in the way the empire was eschatologically perceived.[24] The very future of the church and the well-being of the Roman Empire were inextricably linked, and the rudiments of a Christian account of empire were thereby laid.

Eusebius draws on the vision of peace in Psalm 46:8–9 and proclaims that this has been "clearly fulfilled in our own day" (*Church History* 10.1.5–6). In fact, the effect of Constantine's victory and accession to the imperial throne is itself described in something of an eschatological tone (*Church History* 10.9.7). The reign of God is now universally acknowledged. The whole of society is ordered according to the wisdom of the faith. Since there is one God and one Logos, so there is one emperor, a Christian emperor, and one empire throughout the earth, the imperial microcosm of God's macrocosmic rule and God's kingdom. God is even referred to as "the Author of the empire itself, and of all dominion and power" (*Orations* 3.8). Eusebius continues his praise of the empire using imagery of the ending of tribulation (*Church History* 10.9.9).

Many later critics of this situation argued that the world had mastered the church more than the church mastered the world. First, some believed that, with the influx of members into the church, there emerged the doctrine of the invisibility of the church. No longer could being a Christian be identified with church membership, since many "Christians" in the church clearly had not chosen to follow Christ. Now to be a Christian was transmuted to "inwardness."[25] Second, the church became embroiled in matters of political power, with bishops assuming some judicial and administrative functions. Third, by his active involvement in church affairs, however benevolent, Constantine deprived the church of its independence. He deemed himself not only a divinely appointed ruler of the world but also a *koinos episkopos* (common bishop), that is, a general overseer and

24. Eusebius, *Church History* 10.8.6, in *Nicene and Post-Nicene Fathers*, 2nd series, vol. 1, ed. Philip Schaff, trans. Arthur Cushman (New York: Christian Literature Publishing Co., 1890).

25. John Howard Yoder, *The Priestly Kingdom* (Notre Dame: University of Notre Dame Press, 1984), 136–37.

arbiter of church affairs. Precedent had been set for political rulers' direct involvement in ecclesial affairs, a form of "Caesaropapism."[26] Moreover, while "gladiator games had to be relinquished as too brutal for a Christian society . . . Church leaders had to modify their pacifism in order to allow 'just wars' to defend the Christian empire against the barbarians and infidels who threatened it."[27]

There was often a feeling of Christian discontent with the shifts in ecclesial sensibility and direction. "Even in the fourth-century Christian Empire the present world was by no means a satisfactory place to which to confine one's hopes. It was no Utopia, and the flight to the desert might well offer a welcome way of escape from its oppression and frustrations."[28] The rise of monasticism was, at least in part, a critical response to the changing conditions within the church, and the monastic life became the barometer by which the faithfulness of the church was measured.

Augustine's City of God and the Earthly City

With Augustine, these eschatological concerns with the growing sense of a divinely blessed Christian empire—both the caesaropapism of Eusebius and the papocaesarism of Ambrose's *tempora christiana*—came to a theologically devastating head.

Early in his theological reflections Augustine had been broadly millenarian. For example, he had spoken of the eighth day of resurrection as representing "the new life at the end of the age," while the seventh day represented "the rest and quiet the saints will have on this earth." And so, "the Lord . . . will reign on earth with his saints, as the scriptures say, and he will have his Church here, set apart and purified from all contagious wickedness, with no wicked person coming in."[29]

However, around the late 390s his thinking significantly shifted, so that by the time of Alaric's sacking of Rome on August 24, 410 CE, Augustine

---

26. Hans A. Pohlsander, *The Emperor Constantine*, 2nd ed. (London: Routledge, 1996), 91.

27. Charles Matson Odahl, *Constantine and the Christian Empire* (London: Routledge, 2004), 248.

28. G. W. H. Lampe, "Christian Theology in the Patristic Period," in *A History of Christian Doctrine*, ed. Hubert Cunliffe-Jones (Edinburgh: T&T Clark, 1978), 28.

29. Augustine, *Sermons (230–272B) on Liturgical Seasons*, in *The Works of Saint Augustine: A Translation for the 21st Century*, part III, vol. 7, ed. John E. Rotelle, trans. Edmund Hill (Hyde Park, NY: New City Press, 1993), 175.

"had himself abandoned even moderate millenarian beliefs."[30] So while he spoke around 400 CE of the Sabbath as a type of the promised future rest, the day of sanctification, he did not develop the image in any straightforwardly temporal and millenarian fashion.[31] Instead, these passages show a radical form of reticence by simply refusing to pin the millenarian imagery onto a temporal framework.

The Goths' ransacking of the city came as a deep shock to the Roman imagination and sense of security, even if it "was of greater symbolic than political importance."[32] In its wake Augustine composed his monumental text *The City of God* (written between 413 and 427), with the first ten of the twenty-two books offering an apologetic against those pagans who regarded the sacking of Rome as punishment for the toleration of Christians.

The work is an exploration of "the objects of" a people's "love" or desire, and it is on this basis that Augustine draws a contrast between the earthly city and the city of God.[33] Augustine regards a people's values as indicative of the kind of people they are, and this can be seen in the kinds of gods they worship (*CG* 2.22; 8.17). The immorality of the gods encourages the immorality of their devotees, so that "a battle among divinities, if it really happened, gives excuse for civil wars between men" (*CG* 2.25). Drawing on pagan writers such as Sallust, Varro, Cicero, and Virgil, Augustine develops some particularly trenchant criticisms of the conceit of the imperial project. "Now, to attack one's neighbours, to pass on to crush and subdue more remote peoples without provocation and solely from the thirst for dominion—what is one to call this but brigandage on the grand scale?" (*CG* 4.6). Cain was the first human member of the ungodly city, and he, as the murderer of his brother, becomes in Augustine's account a metaphor of that city (*CG* 14.7.17). The earthly city is a city founded on violence and political ambition, and in Rome's case its very founding myth is itself one of fratricide. Put another way, Roman power is founded on a perpetual state of violence. Accordingly, the Roman imperium's values of peace and justice are not entirely what they appear to be. It is true, Augustine admits, that

---

30. Gerald Bonner, "Augustine and Millenarianism," in *The Making of Orthodoxy: Essays in Honour of Henry Chadwick*, ed. Rowan Williams (Cambridge: Cambridge University Press, 1989), 111.

31. Augustine, Letter 55, 10.19, in *Nicene and Post-Nicene Fathers*, first series, vol. 1, ed. Philip Schaff (New York: Christian Literature Publishing Co., 1886), 309.

32. Henry Chadwick, *Augustine* (Oxford: Oxford University Press, 1986), 97.

33. Augustine, *Concerning the City of God against the Pagans*, trans. Henry Bettensen (Harmondsworth: Penguin Books, 1972), 19.24. Hereafter *CG*.

peace—the ordered harmony of body and soul, and of mind with mind—is the ultimate goal of war, of all politics, indeed of all life (*CG* 19.10–13). But "because God does not rule there the general characteristic of that city is that it is devoid of true justice" (*CG* 19.24). Roman peace is merely the absence of conflict that occurs when the ruler's lust for domination is successful in its conquest, subduing dissent by imposing its own will. Lust for domination and the desire for praise or earthly glory (*CG* 5.12–20) are the common loves that ground Rome as "the capital of the Earthly City" (*CG* 15.5). Instead of virtues, the values of empire are vices (*CG* 19.25). "A people alienated from God must be wretched" (*CG* 19.26).

In contrast, the city of God, to which Christians belong, is an eschatological polity into which we are called by baptism into the church. It is grounded not in the so-called virtues that are founded in violence and inevitably perpetuate violence and domination, but in the grace or gift of God that makes for peace. "The peace of the Heavenly City is a perfectly ordered and perfectly harmonious fellowship in the enjoyment of God, and a mutual fellowship in God" (*CG* 19.13). Hence Christians are good citizens, indeed the only properly good citizens, since it is only in the heavenly city that the true unity of all humanity is restored in the Body of Christ (the church, of which Christ is head) by love.

However, Augustine refuses to simply separate the two cities in some eschatological pessimism over the value of the secular and political. He "does not think—or at least does not consistently think—of two distinct kinds of human association, the sacred and the secular, or even the private and the public. His concern is with the goal of human life as such."[34] For a start, his conception of the city of God provides a mirror in which to view and understand the ways of the empire, founded in what are unmasked as disordered desires that are ultimately damagingly destructive.

Moreover, Augustine refuses to set a pure church in time over against the ways of the world, as would befit Donatists.[35] It is true that he develops the Donatist Tyconius's interpretation of Revelation 20:7 as indicating the present church (*CG* 20.7). "The Church, then, begins its reign with Christ now in the living and the dead" (*CG* 20.9). However, he resists any notion of an eschatologically realized and purified church in the here and now. Put

---

34. Williams, *On Augustine*, 110.

35. In North Africa, the Donatists refused to accept the sacramental authority and leadership of clergy who had denied the Christian faith during the Great Persecution in the early fourth century.

most starkly, the two cities are bound up together "until they are separated by the final judgment" (CG 18.54), and consequently there can be no final separation other than that which God's consummating work provides (CG 1.35). In many ways, then, Augustine speaks of the church as an eschatological reality, as that which is yet to come but nonetheless overlaps with the earthly city. The task of God's people in time is to be "God's chosen means to bring citizens into his Kingdom."[36] In that way, "the future Kingdom of God . . . should begin and develop on earth."[37]

Finally, in this context, despite the strong critical reservations Augustine has about the moral value of the empire, he does not devalue it entirely. Since desire is being reordered in and by the work of God, especially through the church as the instrument of divine giving in the world, he cannot give up hoping for the state. It can, at its best, serve to minimize disorder by restricting the worst effects of our disordered or sinful condition until the consummation, when God will finally separate the "saved and the damned," rewarding the saved but leaving the damned to suffer "the natural, painful effect of sin" in eternal punishment.[38]

Augustine refuses to speculate on the timing of the last judgment. In fact, he even refuses to find discernible patterns in world occurrences whereby any confident assertions can be offered regarding the pattern of divine action in the course of events. "At many points in the work the argument is designed to show how hard it is to discern such a pattern."[39] He observes in a letter of 418 to Hesychius, the bishop of Salonia, that Matthew 12:41–42 teaches only two things: "that there is a judgment to come; and that it will coincide with the resurrection of the dead." Jesus's claim that no one knows the time of the end (Matt. 24:36; Mark 13:32) is a warning even to those who want to perform such eschatological calculations. Augustine admits: "I choose rather to confess a cautious ignorance than to profess a false knowledge."[40] The Danielic language of "weeks" does not, as Jerome pointed out, and Augustine may well agree, refer to the future coming of Christ but rather to his "first" appearance. No matter what, "we pass through this world as pilgrims

36. Mary T. Clark, Augustine (London: Geoffrey Chapman, 1994), 100.

37. Clark, Augustine, 103.

38. Daley, "Eschatology in the Early Fathers," 101; Daley, The Hope of the Early Church, 140.

39. Chadwick, Augustine, 106.

40. Augustine, "Augustine to Bishop Hesychius, On the End of the World" (Letter 197), in Saint Augustine: Letters, vol. 4, The Fathers of the Church 30, trans. Wilfrid Parsons (Washington, DC: Catholic University Press of America, 1955), 350.

while our heart constantly expands with this love [of God], and whether He comes sooner or later than He is expected, His coming is loved with faithful charity and longed for with pious affection."[41] We are to watch at all times, imitating the Apostles "by preparing our heart," and to preach the gospel to the ends of the earth.[42] "Therefore, it is not the one who asserts that He is near nor the one who asserts that He is not near who loves the coming of the Lord, but the one who waits for Him, whether He be near or far, with sincere faith, firm hope and ardent love."[43]

Among other things, the way the images of cities are developed in terms of *desire* crucially enables Augustine to reject the Manichean and Platonic separation of matter from spirit. For the bishop of Hippo, the materiality of the world is not itself the problem. The world is the fruit of God's good giving. It is inordinate and misshapen human desire (or sinfulness) that distorts the world and the things in it to destructive ends. Unsurprisingly, then, Augustine emphasizes the embodied nature of the resurrection and of the condition of the resurrected life. "Our hope is the resurrection of the dead, our faith is the resurrection of the dead. . . . If faith in the resurrection of the dead is taken away, all Christian doctrine perishes. . . . If the dead do not rise, we have no hope of a future life; but if the dead do rise, there *will* be a future life."[44] In fact, his hope is that "the saints will in the resurrection inhabit those very bodies in which they have here toiled" (*CG* 13.19). Moreover, he postulates a period of purgation for those entering the beatific vision, prior to the last judgment.

At the close of *The City of God*, Augustine offers a vision of eternal life: "There we shall be still and see; we shall see and we shall love; we shall love and we shall praise" (*CG* 22.30). Human beings are created for the knowledge and love of God, and it is in the consummated conditions of what he calls the "beatific vision," a vision that he even strains to suggest will be seen with our bodily eyes (*CG* 22.29), that this final flourishing of humanity's created nature within the redemptive purposes of God is realized. This is the anticipated final or last judgment, in which the righteous will gain that for which they have been redeemed, in contrast to the unrighteous, for whom separation and punishment wait. Augustine's account of the separation of heaven and hell, the saved and the unrepentant wicked, is grounded in an

41. Augustine, "To Hesychius, On the End of the World" (Letter 199), in *Saint Augustine: Letters*, vol. 4, 357.

42. Augustine, "To Hesychius, On the End of the World," 362.

43. Augustine, "To Hesychius, On the End of the World," 367.

44. Augustine, *Sermon* 361.2, quoted by Daley, *The Hope of the Early Church*, 139-40.

account of justice, and he even maintains that the image of the fires of hell is to be understood literally.

Political Messianisms

The seventeenth century was an important period for the progress of millenarianism in both the English and the North American contexts in particular, and millenarian approaches played an important role in the political life and imagination of the time. "For many puritans, eschatology was an applied rather than an abstract subject, a cultural as well as a political conflict in which one was automatically involved."[45] While only a few, such as the Fifth Monarchists, engaged in violent action in order to destabilize governments in the 1650s and 1660s, "the seeds of [the English Parliamentarian] revolution were sown in the slow and cautious formation of evangelical millennial belief."[46] It is this political connection and context that is the reason for considering these developments in chapter 3 rather than chapter 1, although the two really cannot be easily separated. This period was so significant for the shaping and reshaping of Christian hope that it "swept away [Protestants'] latent Augustinianism. Later seventeenth-century commentators constructed enduring paradigms of evangelical millennial belief. Those millennial positions that did not conform to these . . . paradigms were increasingly regarded as eccentric."[47]

The English Reformation

In authorizing the publication of an English version of the Bible, Henry VIII "had been mainly concerned to secure England's political independence from the papacy."[48] It was a crucial part of the struggle to establish the world's first wholly self-contained nation-state under the rule of the monarch, with the monarch coming in due time to exercise something approximating to ab-

---

45. Crawford Gribben, *Evangelical Millennialism in the Trans-Atlantic World, 1500–2000* (Basingstoke: Palgrave Macmillan, 2011), 47.
46. Gribben, *Evangelical Millennialism in the Trans-Atlantic World*, 49.
47. Gribben, *Evangelical Millennialism in the Trans-Atlantic World*, 49.
48. Christopher Hill, *The English Bible and the Seventeenth-Century Revolution* (London: Allen Lane, 1993), quoted in Clifford Longley, *Chosen People: The Big Idea That Shapes England and America* (London: Hodder & Stoughton, 2002), 65.

solute rule through divine right. With the help of Thomas Cromwell (1485–1540), King Henry (1491–1547) declared that England had always been free of papal control as a sovereign Christian state. During the preparation of the main acts of government that brought the English church under the control of the crown, Cromwell inserted a historical preamble that rewrote English history so as to suggest that Henry VIII was not an innovator but instead someone faithful to the long and distinctive history of the English church.

At first the notion of a chosen people—the "elect" in Calvin's terms—was understood to have a transnational reference. But the ideology of Henricianism focused the term to apply to England's role to the exclusion of others, such as we find in the theo-historical narrative devised by John Bale (1495–1563). Members of other nations might be among the elect, but there was only one chosen nation, one place where the true gospel had been providentially preserved since the time of Christ—England. Increasingly, England was likened to, and even occasionally identified with, Israel through a nationalist reading of the Old Testament. Henry VIII, and even Oliver Cromwell later, were depicted as Moses leading God's chosen people out of bondage to the Promised Land.

What is particularly noticeable is the way millenarian perspectives developed in this context. During the English Reformation, the more apocalyptic version of eschatological expectation became muted, replaced instead by a perspective that was particularly well-suited to the new political and ecclesiastical conditions. The Church of England's Forty-Two Articles of Religion in 1552 had ruled that millenarianism was unacceptable Anglican teaching. What emerged was a perspective that justified the existence of the Church of England. The rewriting of English national identity by John Foxe (1516–1587), however, came to take a distinctly millenarian turn. His lengthy *Actes and Monuments*, also known as the *Book of Martyrs* (1563), which was composed during the reign of Queen Elizabeth I, associates the enemies of England with the enemies of freedom, the Bible, and God. Appealing to the book of Revelation, Foxe uses striking rhetoric against the unholy enemy, describing the place of England in the redemptive work of God against the Antichrist (the pope) under the Christian emperor (Queen Elizabeth). In other words, he provides a rereading of the apocalyptic version of English history and rejection of the papacy as the Antichrist, both of which were adopted from Foxe's friend John Bale. The enemies Foxe refers to were idolatrous, superstitious, cruel, tyrannical, and above all *foreign*, just like the enemies of ancient Israel—the pharaohs of Egypt, the Babylonian kings, and so on. The revised editions of *Actes and Monuments* even contain tables speculating on the numerological significance of the numbers provided by Revelation.

English Puritanism

The passing of royal succession from Henry VIII to Edward VI began to swing English politics sharply. Radical Protestants took their objections to the Roman version of Christianity much further than the Henrician quarrel over papal jurisdiction had done. Queen Mary Tudor's persecution of them—many fled into exile in Lutheran Germany and Calvinist Switzerland—radicalized a Protestant anti-Anglicanism that was politically republican and egalitarian in matters of ecclesiastical organization.

Later, in 1633, William Laud, the Archbishop of Canterbury, banned all publications that identified Rome or the papacy as the Antichrist.[49] But efforts to mute the millenarian perspective during the reigns of Edward, Elizabeth, and James nonetheless began to unravel in the early seventeenth century. Influenced particularly by the growing apocalypticism of Martin Luther, in his later years, and Heinrich Bullinger, the Puritans expressed their anti-Catholic worry about the threat of "popery" in apocalyptic terms, and they expressed a sense of the impending fulfillment of millenarian hopes in which "a holy commonwealth could be established on earth."[50]

It was not long after Charles I's enthronement that Joseph Mede published his *Clavis Apocalyptica* (1627). On the one hand, his eschatological perspective is informed by a certain sense of theological modesty: "we shall . . . enquire in vaine of those things which God would have kept secret and to be reserved for their owne times."[51] Yet, on the other hand, he develops a millenarian reading of Revelation 20, which is unpacked in terms of a chronological mapping of the various visions onto a set of specific historical fulfillments. One of a group of Protestant apocalypticists for whom Laud's Catholic reforms of the Church of England were regarded as a heinous betrayal of the gospel, he declared the Roman Catholic Church and the papacy

49. Jeffrey K. Jue, "Puritan Millenarianism in Old and New England," in *The Cambridge Companion to Puritanism*, ed. John Coffey and Paul C. H. Lim (Cambridge: Cambridge University Press, 2008), 264.

50. Larzer Ziff, *The Career of John Cotton: Puritanism and the American Experience* (Princeton: Princeton University Press, 1962), 156.

51. Mede, *The Key of the Revelation*, 1.21, quoted in Gribben, *Evangelical Millennialism in the Trans-Atlantic World*, 49.

to be demonic institutions. In fact, the cult of saints had been predicted in 1 Timothy 4:1 as the great apostasy of the latter times. The fall of the Antichrist would occur prior to the inauguration of God's millenarian rule.

It was precisely such apocalyptically designed millenarian sentiment that was accentuated during this tumultuous political period, and it "provided a theological context in which to frame decisive political and military action."[52] Millenarians of the period anticipated the fulfillment of Daniel 7's prophecy that, after four successive earthly monarchies were destroyed, a fifth godly monarchy would be established, a final monarchy frequently equated with the millennium of Revelation 20.[53] With the execution of Charles I in 1649, the collapse of the Antichrist and the coming of God's millenarian kingdom began to look imminent.

New England

However, in 1660, with the Restoration and the crowning of Charles II, Puritan rule in England abruptly ended. Over a thousand Puritan ministers were expelled from their pulpits as a result of the Act of Uniformity of 1662. Many journeyed to the Americas in the Puritan "errand into the wilderness," taking with them a millenarian version of Puritan faith, a need for refuge, and a sense that the "old world" was corrupt and decadent.[54] Thomas Brightman (1562–1607), for instance, associated the Church of England with the Laodicean church in Revelation 3:14–22 as a consequence of the Elizabethan settlement, the curtailing of ecclesial reform by James I, and the ecclesiastical developments by William Laud. Writing to Mede, William Twisse pondered whether North America could be the location of the New Jerusalem, even though Mede himself was deeply unimpressed and regarded the Americas as the domain of Satan. Some certainly interpreted God's redemptive action through their work in millenarian terms, with New England becoming a microcosm of God's kingdom, "a preview of the New Jerusalem."[55] One common feature of the colonial Puritans' theology was their typological use of the Old Testament image of Israel (specifically as a nation in cove-

---

52. Jue, "Puritan Millenarianism in Old and New England," 264–65.

53. Jue, "Puritan Millenarianism in Old and New England," 266.

54. Perry Miller, *Errand into the Wilderness* (Cambridge, MA: Belknap Press of Harvard University Press, 1956).

55. Sacvan Bercovitch, "Typology in Puritan New England: The Williams-Cotton Controversy Reassessed," *American Quarterly* 19, no. 2 (1967): 175.

nant with God). In their accounts, just as Israel traveled from bondage in Egypt, through the wilderness, and finally arrived at the Promised Land, so these early Puritans journeyed from bondage to the Promised Land of North America.[56] The settlers seemingly believed America to be the "new Canaan" and "Promised Land" from which the millennium would emerge.[57]

Referring explicitly to the New World, John Winthrop declared in his sermon of 1630, "A Modell of Christian Charity," that the colonies would be a "city upon a hill" for the rest of the world to notice, observe, and admire.[58] Certainly Winthrop was careful not to provide a geo-political location for the coming of God's new world. In fact, he warned his audience that if they lived falsely, divine favor would be withdrawn, resulting in the New Englanders becoming only a story and a by-word throughout the world.

Among the most prominent millenarians were the likes of John Cotton (1585–1652), John Eliot (1604–1690), Peter Bulkeley (1583–1659), and Increase Mather (1639–1723). Influenced by Thomas Brightman, the eminent clergyman John Cotton, an immigrant to Massachusetts who fled conditions of anti-Puritanism in England, was the first to preach explicitly on millenarian themes from the book of Revelation in New England. While Cotton refused to separate from the Church of England, he did at least inherit an agenda from Brightman that furnished the desire to restore the church to the faithfulness of an earlier time, and he also applied this hope to the English nation itself. Cotton believed that there were demonstrable signs of success in the church's resistance of the Antichrist and the beast, or the papacy and Rome respectively, and that God's wrath was therefore being poured out on wickedness. Developing a scheme of salvation history adapted from the image of the seven vials in the book of Revelation, he claimed that four vials had already been poured out before Charles I's accession—two of them during the reign of Elizabeth. Accordingly, he argued, "you will finde little difference between Episcopacy and Popery, for they are governed by Popish Canons."[59] Living in the period in which the fifth vial would be poured out,

56. Jue argues, however, that they did not imagine that they *replaced* Israel in any supercessionist way. Jue, "Puritan Millenarianism in Old and New England," 271.

57. Michael Northcott, *An Angel Directs the Storm: Apocalyptic Religion and American Empire* (London: I. B. Tauris & Co., 2004), 14-21.

58. John Winthrop, "A Modell of Christian Charity," text in the Collections of the Massachusetts Historical Society (Boston, 1838), 3rd ser., 7:31–48, quoted in Geoffrey Hodgson, *The Myth of American Exceptionalism* (New Haven: Yale University Press, 2009), 1.

59. John Cotton, *The churches resurrection* (London, 1642), 19, quoted in Gribben, *Evangelical Millennialism in the Trans-Atlantic World*, 47.

Cotton regarded the recovery of the church to lie ahead. The advent of the millennium and the New Jerusalem on earth, what Brightman had called the "golden age," would occur once the Antichrist and "Romish" corruption had been defeated.[60]

The Destiny of Secular Millenarianism

This ideology morphed into a "secular" political millenarianism with a national sense of destiny for the building of the holy commonwealth, the "new world." The theme of the people as a type of Israel eventually became a foundational block in the consciousness of many Americans, who believed they were a divinely chosen *independent* people. In this context, George Washington was eventually portrayed in the role of Moses. As news of the British bombardment of Boston in 1774 reached Philadelphia, the Episcopalian Jacob Duche preached a homily that explicated Psalm 35 in such a way as to unambiguously enlist the biblical story of God's people on America's side in the coming struggle.[61] Likewise, Herman Melville wrote, "We Americans are the peculiar, chosen people—the Israel of our time; we bear the ark of the liberties of the world. . . . Long enough have we been skeptics with regard to ourselves, and doubted whether, indeed, the political Messiah had come. But he has come in us, if we would but give utterance to his promptings."[62]

A little later, Julia Ward Howe's 1861 "Battle Hymn of the Republic" connected national destiny and violent action, and particularly the cause of the nation with the redemptive cause of God. This anthem develops apocalyptic biblical imagery through an implicit reference to the Union armies as "the coming of the Lord," their vengeance being "where the grapes of wrath are stored." Their cause is "God's righteous sentence," and in place of the gospel of peacemaking comes the fiery gospel "writ in burnished rows of steel."

In this vein, the frontier narrative became important, with its sense of an uncivilized and barbarically destructive native who threatens the morally pure settlers. It is this rhetoric that underlay "Manifest Destiny and the allegedly selfless imperialism of earlier American civil religion, when seizing other coun-

---

60. Brightman, quoted in Katharine R. Firth, *Apocalyptic Tradition in Reformation Britain, 1530–1645* (Oxford: Oxford University Press, 1969), 174.

61. George W. Bush alluded to both Ps. 35:5 and Duche's use of it when speaking of "angels in the wind" in his inaugural address.

62. Herman Melville, *White-Jacket; or, The World in a Man-of-War* (1850; Evanston: Northwestern University and Newberry Library, 1970), 151.

tries surfaced as the nation's mission during the Spanish-American War."[63] The so-called myth of American exceptionalism has led to the widespread American (religio-political) "secular" belief that American national self-interest is identical with global altruism, so that "what was good for America was good for the world," and the nation was to be the global moral leader.[64]

Jürgen Moltmann's Theology of Hope

By the 1960s postwar Europe had moved beyond the pressing and immediate task of reconstruction and renewal that had occupied the prior decade and a half, and into a period characterized by hope for the future. Between 1962 and 1965 the Second Vatican Council met with the task of modernizing the church, *aggiornamento*, and in 1968 the World Council of Churches' conference on hope convened in Uppsala. In the United States, protests for civil rights erupted, calling for social and political justice and for a system of equity. Christian and Marxist conversations from West and East Germany began to take place in earnest, particularly through the inspiration of philosopher Ernst Bloch, and Ernst Käsemann encouraged a focus on eschatological matters among New Testament scholars.

"The eschatological vision becomes operative, the theology of hope becomes creative, when it comes into contact with the social realities of today's world and gives rise to what has been called 'political theology.'"[65] With these words Gustavo Gutiérrez (1928–) refers to the direction provided by Johann Baptist Metz (1928–), who "attempts to show the implications of eschatology and hope for political life." Resisting the (bourgeois) privatizing of Christian faith in the secularizing market economies, Metz announced that "it is impossible to privatize the eschatological promises of biblical tradition. Again and again they force us to assume our responsibilities towards society."[66]

---

63. Robert Jewett and John Shelton Lawrence, *Captain America and the Crusade against Evil: The Dilemma of Zealous Nationalism* (Grand Rapids: Eerdmans, 2003), 30–31.

64. John Fousek, *To Lead the Free World: American Nationalism and the Cultural Roots of the Cold War* (Chapel Hill: University of North Carolina Press, 2000), quoted in Trevor McCrisken and Andrew Pepper, *American History and Contemporary Hollywood Film* (Edinburgh: Edinburgh University Press, 2005), 120.

65. Gustavo Gutiérrez, *A Theology of Liberation: History, Politics, and Salvation*, trans. Caridad Inda and John Eagleson (London: SCM, 1974), 205.

66. Johann Baptist Metz, *Theology of the World*, trans. William Glen-Doepel (New York: Herder and Herder, 1969), 114.

Among other things, hope provides an "eschatological proviso," a critical perspective that refuses the finalization of any and every political and economic system and activity. Eschatology requires the perspective that every historical activity is provisional. That enables the eschatological imagination to necessarily become "a critical liberating imperative for our present times."[67]

The necessary political outworking of hope became most apparent in the theology of the second half of the twentieth century in the work of Jürgen Moltmann. Moltmann's *Theology of Hope* not only generated enough attention so as to enable hope to remain a vital stream of theological conversation in the second half of the century, but also made a name for the young German theologian.

Having been a prisoner of war from 1945 to 1948 in Belgium, Scotland, and England, Moltmann identified two themes that were crucial in his experience: the experience of God as the power of the promise of hope, and the experience of God's presence in solidarity to sufferers. Published at a time of buoyant hope for the future of Europe after its postwar rebuilding, his book reflected the influence of, among others, the Jewish Marxist philosopher Ernst Bloch's three-volume *The Principle of Hope*, and through him Karl Marx (1818–1883), during a period of significant Christian-Marxist conversations. Moltmann's book is not a systematic discussion of eschatological matters as much as a methodological reflection on hope, a proclamation of the eschatological orientation of all theology, and an eschatological redescription of appropriate Christian practice. Driving the work is a sense that the young Barth had been right to criticize the dislocation of eschatology from other doctrinal loci such as the doctrine of God, Christology, soteriology, pneumatology, and so on. Such a dislocation does not merely impoverish Christian theology but actually distorts it. Moltmann therefore echoed the early Barth's claim: "From first to last, and not merely in the epilogue, Christianity is eschatology. . . . The eschatological is not one element *of* Christianity, but is the medium of Christian faith as such, the key in which everything is set, the glow that suffuses everything here in the dawn of an unexpected new day."[68]

Moltmann works this out through an eschatological "rediscovery" of *history* in the eschatological purposes of God. "Christian eschatology speaks

67. Metz, *Theology of the World*, 114.

68. Jürgen Moltmann, *Theology of Hope: On the Ground and the Implications of a Christian Eschatology*, trans. Margaret Kohl (London: SCM, 1967), 16. Hereafter *TH*. See also Karl Barth, *The Epistle to the Romans*, trans. of the 6th ed. by Edwyn C. Hoskyns (Oxford: Oxford University Press, 1968), 314.

of God historically, and of history eschatologically."[69] God draws creation, the whole of creation no less, toward its singularly purposed end, an end that had been promised and anticipated by God's creative and saving works, especially in Israel's Messiah. This makes Jesus Christ, crucified and raised, "the precursor, the place-holder, and the representative of the coming of God" (HH, 379). Hope operates here within a "promise-fulfillment" scheme of salvation history for the entirety of history, "one universal future for all men and all things" (HH, 372). Putting things in such a way necessitates that Christian hope "does not speak of the future as such. It sets out from a definite reality in history and announces the future of that reality, its future possibilities and its power over the future. Christian eschatology speaks of Jesus Christ and *his* future" (*TH*, 17). Christ, then, is not limited to being simply the first fruits of the general resurrection of the dead to new life but is rather "the source of the risen life of all believers" (*TH*, 83).

The universal scope of God's eschatological work raises the question of the restoration of all things (*apokatastasis pantōn*). Moltmann is hopeful, but he nonetheless is reticent to proclaim a cosmic consummation. "Eschatology is not a doctrine about history's happy end. . . . No one can assure us that the worst will not happen. We can only trust that even the end of the world hides a new beginning if we trust the God who calls into being the things that are not, and out of death creates new life."[70] In a paper on the theological issue of hell, Moltmann declares that "the logic of hell seems to me not merely inhumane but also extremely atheistic: here the human being in his freedom of choice is his own lord and god."[71]

Among other things, this allows him to distinguish eschatological hope, the *adventus* or coming of God, from utopian hopes. Eschatology does not speak of the future as such, but rather the future of God's reality in Christ. That means that "in the person and history of Jesus Christ [God] provides . . . the touchstone by which to distinguish the spirit of eschatology from that of utopia" (*TH*, 17). Eschatology has to do with the *new* possibility, the *novum* given by God's action. This is not the new *in* history, as if God provides one of many new possibilities, but rather the new that comes to, includes, and thereby transforms history.

69. Jürgen Moltmann, "Hope and History," *Theology Today* 25, no. 3 (1968): 372. Hereafter HH.

70. Jürgen Moltmann, *The Coming of God: Christian Eschatology*, trans. Margaret Kohl (London: SCM, 1996), 234. Hereafter CG.

71. Jürgen Moltmann, "The Logic of Hell," in *God Will Be All in All: The Eschatology of Jürgen Moltmann*, ed. Richard Bauckham (Edinburgh: T&T Clark, 1999), 45.

This is where Moltmann departs from Barth. Barth, along with Bultmann, is regarded by him as having inappropriately remolded eschatology
into the thought forms of the Greek traditions during the time of the early
church, emphasizing the epiphany of the eternal in the present. For Barth,
revelation is the detemporalized presence of the self-revelation of God; while
for Bultmann, what is emphasized is the transcendental subjectivity of the
solitary human in faith.

Moltmann builds a future dynamic into his account of God so that all
things are "eschatologically directed toward the future of God" (HH, 375).
On the one hand, he offers the image of the future *of* God in order to depict
the universal realization or manifestation or reality of "the coming of his
unlimited reign" (HH, 376). God is not as yet present in the form of God's
eternal presence, which fills and fulfills all things. This future is the future
in which God comes to gloriously indwell God's creation unrestrictedly and
unmediatedly, the creation fulfilled and transformed by participating in the
divine life in "a mutual indwelling of the world in God and God in the
world" through the resurrection of the dead (*CG*, 307). Moltmann depicts
this indwelling through the images of God's Sabbath rest and cosmic Shekinah presence. On the other hand, the image has an ontological function.
As mentioned above, "Christian eschatology *speaks of God historically*, and
of history eschatologically" (HH, 372, emphasis added). Accordingly, God
comes to God's creatures *from the future.*[72]

Moltmann's work has often been particularly celebrated for his manner
of working out the implications of his account ethically and politically, as
hope for this world and not for another. As he argues, "The theologian is
not concerned merely to supply a different *interpretation* of the world, of
history and of human nature, but to *transform* them in expectation of a
divine transformation" (*TH*, 84). "Eschatology is generally held to be the
doctrine of 'the Last Things', or of 'the end of all things'. To think this is to
think in good apocalyptic terms, but it is not understanding eschatology in
the Christian sense" (*CG*, x–xi).

The apocalyptic form of eschatology, then, with its "question about the
end," "bursts out of the torrent of history and the intolerableness of historical existence." Moltmann does not take this particular direction, and in his
later work he even develops a form of millenarianism while reinterpreting
the ancient notion of hell. "*Christian* eschatology has nothing to do with

---

72. Jürgen Moltmann, "My Theological Career," in *History and the Triune God: Contributions to Trinitarian Theology* (London: SCM, 1991), 169.

apocalyptic 'final solutions' of this kind, for its subject is not 'the end' at all. On the contrary, what it is about is the new creation of all things." Working in this way presses him to, among other things, critique the debt society, the threat of nuclear annihilation, and the ecological crisis, all of which mortally threaten life on this planet, as Christians work to bring the "hoped-for future into the sufferings of the present age." He interrogates and contests the instrumentalization of life in industrial societies, the defining of the value of human life in terms of production and consumption, the individualization and privatization of human self-understanding and existence, and the complicity of the churches with the powerful. "God's 'kingdom' and 'righteousness' are alternative visions to everything we experience here and now as human Realpolitik or power politics, and as injustice and the oppression of the weak in our society."[73]

Moltmann's ethics of hope for the liberative renewing of the world is grounded in the resurrection of Christ in such a way that theology is necessarily "political theology." What this means is that the horizon of the eschatological coming of God "already qualifies the present" (HH, 376). Hope is hope for all things, and it cannot leave anything or anyone unhoped for: "its healing future embraces every individual and the whole universe. If we were to surrender hope for as much as one single creature, for us God would not be God" (CG, 132).

Liberation Theologies

Major factors in the development of "liberation theology," a name coined by Peruvian priest Gustavo Gutiérrez in his classic A Theology of Liberation in 1971, were the positions on justice and peace taken by Roman Catholicism and various branches of Protestantism in the 1950s and 1960s, the conversations between Christians and Marxists, and the development of political theologies. Most important among these developments was the social teaching of Vatican II concerning human dignity and the need for structural change. Latin American bishops met in Medellín, Colombia, in 1968 to discuss the implications of Vatican II for Latin America, and the papers adopted by the bishops became the founding documents of liberation theology. At Medellín, the struggle for change that would guide liberation theology was begun, a

---

73. Jürgen Moltmann, "Hope and Reality: A Contradiction and Correspondence," in Bauckham, God Will Be All in All, 78.

struggle against the institutionalized violence suffered by the poor as a result of a worldwide imperialism of money, represented by the upper classes and foreign monopolies, and the dependency enforced on the poor. A vision of faith was articulated from the viewpoint of the poor as human subjects active in history. This vision was located in small grassroots communities where the poor could determine their own destiny and express their faith as they participated in conscientization or consciousness-raising.

In their introduction to liberation theology, after identifying a range of forms of unjust suffering in Latin America, Leonardo (1938–) and Clodovis Boff (1944–) explain that "underlying liberation theology is a prophetic and comradely commitment to the life, cause, and struggle of these millions of debased and marginalized human beings, a commitment to ending this historical-social inequity."[74] After all, "misery is not innocent. It does not come out of nowhere."[75] Sin is not, and cannot be, reducible to an interior or private problem. Real poverty "is a situation wholly contrary to the will of God."[76] The term "liberation theology," then, should be understood as an umbrella term for theology protesting against the systems that generate and maintain injustice, oppression, and enforced poverty and working for transformation for suffering peoples as the necessary outworking of a vision of the world's new life in Christ. Witnessing to suffering, therefore, is problematic unless it emerges from, and is bound to, "effective action for liberation"; the Suffering Servant who was crucified "needs to be raised to life" (*ILT*, 4). In this regard, liberation theologies demand radical transformation and not a reformism or a developmentalism that maintains the existing social, economic, and political power structures.

Marxist forms of analysis have been particularly instructive in deep analyses of the phenomenon of oppression. This does not mean that liberation theologies are Marxist theologies as such. Rather, Boff and Boff maintain, "liberation theology uses Marxism purely as an *instrument*. It does not venerate it as it venerates the gospel" (*ILT*, 28). This entails that liberation theologies are not political programs insulated from, or simply supple-

74. Leonardo Boff and Clodovis Boff, *Introducing Liberation Theology*, trans. Paul Burns (Tunbridge Wells: Burns & Oates, 1987), 3. Hereafter *ILT*.

75. Leonardo Boff, "Salvation in Liberation: The Theological Meaning of Socio-Historical Liberation," in Leonardo Boff and Clodovis Boff, *Salvation and Liberation: In Search of a Balance between Faith and Politics*, trans. Robert R. Barr (Quezon City: Claretian Publications, 1985), 4.

76. Gustavo Gutiérrez, "The Task and Content of Liberation Theology," trans. Judith Condor, in *The Cambridge Companion to Liberation Theology*, ed. Christopher Rowland (Cambridge: Cambridge University Press, 1999), 25.

mented by, theological critique. According to Gutiérrez, "The theology of liberation, like any theology, is about God. God and love are, ultimately, its only theme."[77] Rather, Marxist analysis can operate as a witness to the praxis of faith, to the radical demands that embody the pressure of the gospel for the holistic healing of life. "Social sin must be opposed by social grace, fruit of God's gift and of human endeavor inspired by God" (ILT, 62). In other words, "these practices"—the preferential option for, and solidarity with, the poor as a way of life, or resistance and transformative social struggle—"are demanded by the Christian faith itself."[78]

Implicitly addressing Marx's critique of Christian hope, Boff and Boff assert that "Christianity can no longer be dismissed as the opium of the people, nor can it be seen as merely fostering an attitude of critique: it has now become an active commitment to liberation" (ILT, 7). Nonetheless, the churches have frequently supported the status quo, being "bound to the dominant classes," and therefore they have embodied relations of power that are inappropriate to this theologically transformative demand.[79] So Leonardo Boff laments, "The church came to the aid of the poor, it is true, but made no use of the resources of the poor in instituting a process of change."[80]

Among a number of biblical images that play an important role in theologies of liberation is that of the exodus. The exodus reveals, not a "spiritual" God who is merely to be contemplated, but a liberating God acting on behalf of the manipulated and oppressed communities. "The living God takes sides against the pharaohs of this world . . . [o]ut of love for" the oppressed (ILT, 50–51). Another image is that of the prophetic mission of the people of God in proclaiming the coming of God's reign of peace, justice, and freedom, which simultaneously involves the punishment of the oppressors.[81] Finally, liberation theologies utilize eschatological imagery in order to indicate the shape of hope for the healing brought by God's redemptive liberation. So Gutiérrez proclaims that "the conquest of misery and the abolition of exploitation are signs of the Messiah's arrival. . . . To fight for a just world where there is no servitude, oppression, or alienated work is to proclaim and signify the advent of the Messiah."[82]

77. Gutiérrez, "The Task and Content of Liberation Theology," 19.
78. Leonardo Boff, "Salvation in Liberation," 4.
79. Leonardo Boff, "Salvation in Liberation," 3.
80. Leonardo Boff, "Salvation in Liberation," 3.
81. Gustavo Gutiérrez, "Creating a New Ecclesial Presence," in Gustavo Gutiérrez: Essential Writings, ed. James B. Nickoloff (Minneapolis: Fortress, 1996), 239.
82. Gutiérrez, "Creating a New Ecclesial Presence," 239.

Reflecting on the Gospel of Mark's use of the term *kairos* rather than *chronos* in order to depict the time of fulfillment, Gutiérrez argues "that God is now being revealed in a special way in the history in which Jesus has involved himself."[83] This is something he explicates as a way of resisting interiorized, and therefore politically conformist, understandings of the coming of God's kingdom. So he speaks in terms of the finality of God's judgment both as an already manifested gift or "*grace* of God" and as a kairological "*demand* made upon us." This judgment of God announces God's reaction to the state of affairs that exists in contrast to the kingdom, so that the signs of that kingdom may be properly manifest in "gestures of solidarity among the poor" and in the people's struggle for liberation. "The life and preaching of Jesus postulate the unceasing search for a new kind of humanity in a qualitatively different society."[84]

Boff and Boff's particular eschatological vision is one of total actualization or healing, of cosmic purification in the gracious presence of God. It is also something more than any historical liberation, since the latter would always be revisable and provisional, even if it is anticipated in the historical event. "The kingdom or reign of God means the full and total liberation of all creation, in the end, purified of all that oppresses it, transfigured by the full presence of God" (*ILT*, 52). In marked contrast, Juan Luis Segundo (1925–1996) claims that "*the kingdom of God is not announced to everyone. It is not 'proclaimed' to all. . . . The kingdom is destined for certain groups. It is theirs. It belongs to them. Only for them it will cause joy. And, according to Jesus, the dividing line between joy and woe produced by the kingdom runs between the poor and the rich.*"[85] For Boff and Boff, nonetheless, the healing of injustices, the "hope for a reconciled kingdom in which universal peace is the fruit of divine justice and the integration of all things in God," is an eschatological event, and because of the resurrection it is not only to be expected in the consummated future but also "begins to come about in this world" (*ILT*, 54, 52).

What is the role of the church in the triumph of God's eschatological action, in the project of God's kingdom in history? Boff and Boff argue that "under different sacred and profane signs, the kingdom is always present where persons bring about justice, seek comradeship, forgive each other,

83. Gutiérrez, "The Kingdom Is at Hand," in *Gustavo Gutiérrez: Essential Writings*, 173.

84. Gustavo Gutiérrez, *A Theology of Liberation: History, Politics, and Salvation*, trans. Caridad Inda and John Eagleson (London: SCM, 1974), 216.

85. Juan Luis Segundo, *The Historical Jesus of the Synoptics*, trans. John Drury (Mayknoll, NY: Orbis, 1985), 90.

and promote life" (*ILT*, 53). Yet, among other things, the church's structures are inadequate to deal with the deep problems in society and are unable to become sufficiently agile to engage substantially in liberative praxis.[86]

Because of this, liberation theologians tend to emphasize the transformative potential of small "base communities" living out the Christian life of peace and justice in grass-roots cooperation.[87] Working from Matthew 25:31–46, Boff and Boff argue that "those who commune in his history with the poor and needy . . . are Christ's sacraments" (*ILT*, 45). This is an eschatological image of the final judgment: "at the supreme moment of history, when our eternal salvation or damnation will be decided, what will count will be our attitude of acceptance or rejection of the poor." According to Boff and Boff, "the kingdom finds a particular expression in the church, which is its perceptible sign, its privileged instrument" (*ILT*, 53). It is this that makes it the universal sacrament of salvation, the instrument for God's building the kingdom through human actions.[88]

---

86. Gutiérrez, "Creating a New Ecclesial Presence," 237.

87. Base communities were small gatherings, usually outside of churches, in which the Bible could be discussed and mass could be said.

88. See Gutiérrez, *A Theology of Liberation*, ch. 12.

4. Christological

The eschatological imagery of the New Testament grows largely out of the developments of Hebrew faith and life. But its distinctive character is determined by the conviction that, in the life of Jesus, God's decisive eschatological act has already taken place, though in such a way that it has not yet been consummated. It is important to recognize this connection with Hebrew thought and life in Christianity's Christ-centered perspective, since there is an odd reading of the New Testament that sounds, at its worst, as if it has forgotten Christian eschatology's Jewish origins. This problem has taken two main forms.

The first form is one in which Christians have come to emphasize a notion of immortality that is largely separated from Christology: an immortality of the *soul* that tends to be contrasted with the physicality and mortality of bodies; a coming life in a space called *heaven* that is other than the life of this world; a waiting for heaven that emphasizes the place of the *individual* in God's eschatological redemption rather than the cosmic or social; and a *waiting* for this heavenly life that emphatically separates God's action from human action.

A second form suggests that the history of early Christian theology is the gradual distortion of the original message, and that there are hints of various levels of this distortion in the New Testament's eschatology itself. According to this perspective, reading the New Testament appropriately for today must identify and reinterpret these ideas.

The Eschatological Presence of Christ in the New Testament

The "Delay" of the Parousia

It is clear that many early Christian communities did not confess the approaching—and soon to be arriving—kingdom of God as some abstract or general entity. Instead, they made two quite startling moves. First, they connected the sense of the eschatological presence of God to the creativity of God, so that all things are drawn into the coming of God's work of redemptive renewal. Second, quite early on, they were beginning to identify this divine creativity and re-creativity as somehow bound up in, by, and through Jesus the Christ as "the agent of eschatological salvation" (in fact, as the very agent of God's judgment).[1] Just how early this occurred remains a matter of scholarly dispute, but Colossians 1:15-20, which could be part of an earlier hymn, strikingly admits that "in him all things in heaven and on earth were created . . . all things have been created through him and for him" (Col. 1:16). This echo of the Wisdom tradition (see Wis. 7:25-26) equates Jesus as the presence of God's own Wisdom, so that "Christ had already in Paul's time begun to attract to himself, perhaps half-consciously, the language normally appropriate for God."[2] The prologue or "overture to the [Fourth] Gospel in which its main themes are announced" is the most developed version of this, with the concept of God's preexistent Word being depicted likewise through imagery used in the Wisdom literature for Wisdom herself.[3] These passages are sometimes described as offering a "high Christology," and that is certainly true. But the texts also irreducibly offer a "high" view of creation and of the end of that creation in Christ (see Rev. 1:17). This is especially noteworthy given the various pressures these communities were under from philosophies in their religious surroundings that would later flower as full-blown dualisms.

A further matter needs to be noticed as well, and that is the mood of the New Testament in the face of the increasing "delay of the *parousia*." If scholars such as Martin Werner are right, this deferral was a significant feature in the development of the early Christian theological imagina-

---

1. Christopher Rowland, "The Eschatology of the New Testament Church," in *The Oxford Handbook of Eschatology*, ed. Jerry L. Walls (Oxford: Oxford University Press, 2008), 58.

2. J. H. Houlden, *Paul's Letters from Prison: Philippians, Colossians, Philemon and Ephesians* (Harmondsworth: Penguin Books, 1970), 169.

3. George R. Beasley-Murray, *John* (Dallas: Word, 1987), lxxxiii, referring to an image developed from T. E. Pollard. See Prov. 8:22-23; Sir. 24:9; Wis. 6:22.

tion.[4] The "delay" is explicitly referred to in 2 Peter 3:1-10 and 1 Thessalonians 4:13-18, but in the former text it is proclaimed as having its own rationale in God's merciful forbearance, a forbearance that may prove to be long outstanding (see Rom. 2:4). In 1 Thessalonians 5:6, Paul urges the Christians to be "alert and self-controlled." In 2 Thessalonians 3:6-13 he chastises those who have given up living a normal life in view of their expectation of the imminent coming of Christ. This passage lays out "an eschatological program which is intended to diminish the intensity of expectation. . . . Certain things have to take place before Christ will return. Until they do, there is no point in idleness; Christians should carry on with their normal lives and not be carried away with their enthusiasm."[5] Certainly there are three passages in which Jesus himself appears to teach the imminent coming of the *parousia*: Matthew 10:23; Mark 9:1; and Mark 13:30. However, the Markan insistence that we do not know the details of the end may well be a way of restraining any possible sense of disappointment in the church. Again, Luke, the "theologian of the early church's mission," in addition to echoing the Markan reserve (Luke 21:9), undermines the idea of an interim between Jesus's death and his *parousia* by interpreting history in the light of God's history of salvation in Jesus (Luke 1:5; 2:1).

Perhaps the reason for this is that the *terminus* had not come, and the writings themselves were evidence of a readjusting of the expectations of Christian hope. Paul, for instance, on one occasion seems to suggest that the eschaton had already made progress since his conversion (Rom. 13:11), although he shows no sign of anxiety that it still remains outstanding. This relative serenity, however, may well be attributed to his assurance that the "coming of the Lord" would be in his lifetime (1 Thess. 4:15). The question is, was this imminent expectation intrinsic to his faith? His comment that he longs to die and be with the Lord (Phil. 1:23) suggests that it is not, since it implies a different understanding of the eschatological presence of God in Christ. In Christ, God has acted decisively in, on, and for God's people, and through Christ and by the Spirit God is gloriously present. Paul's "hope was bound not to a fixed date but to the gospel that pronounced the fulfillment of the Old Testament promises and called for trusting" God.[6]

---

4. Likewise, see C. H. Dodd, *The Coming of Christ: Four Broadcast Addresses for the Season of Advent* (Cambridge: Cambridge University Press, 1954), 6.

5. Rowland, "The Eschatology of the New Testament Church," 66.

6. Hans Schwarz, "Eschatology," in *Christian Dogmatics*, vol. 2, ed. Carl E. Braaten and Robert W. Jenson (Philadelphia: Fortress, 1984), 498-99.

However, even if this is a possible reading of the New Testament itself, evaluating this reading is difficult. Is the reassessment of the expectation by deferral of the *parousia* a transgressive moment that departs from the sense of the original gospel, or is it instead a realization of precisely the very sense of that original message? The extant material is just too thin to conclude either way. At most one has to reassert that the New Testament's mood is not one of intensively frustrated expectation or unfulfilled hope, and certainly not of despair over the situation. If the delay was a problem for the earliest churches, one might expect to see it reflected more frequently in the Christian writings of the first century.

Crucially, the material insists predominantly on God's new world having already dawned in Jesus Christ, even if there is also the awareness that the kingdom is not yet here in its fullness. Thus there already seems to be in the New Testament an appreciation that the imminent "end" has to do with the presence of God in Christ, and that the urgency of the demand for a faithful response to him has less to do with the world's dawning *temporal* end than with the arrival of the world's *ontological* End or new beginning. The "last days" of the prophets have arrived in Jesus the Christ but have not yet been fulfilled. This stress on judgment having come in Jesus Christ is different in mood from that which developed with people like Justin the Martyr in the mid-second century, with his emphasis on the provisional judgment at death that is followed by the placing of souls in an intermediate state prior to the final or last judgment.

Does this mean that the New Testament does not even teach a temporal *end* to the world? The point above is that the focus is not upon a temporal end at all but upon the *End* who is Christ our hope. That, of course, is not to deny that an end was expected. However, the expectation of a coming completion seems to grow theologically out of a sense of what has *already* occurred, from the promises that suggest there is even more to come. Moreover, this reading of Christ as End *beyond* the end of the world is not a detemporalization of eschatology as such: creatures who live in time may be encountered at all times by God in Christ, by the Christ in whom the kingdom is realized, but this realization is a "not yet" *in them*. In an important sense, then, it remains yet to come. In this way the church still experiences its time as the time between the futurei tion of Jesus and the consummating coming of Christ. This structuring of time in Christ is depicted in, for example, the central historic rite of Christian worship, the Lord's Supper or Eucharist (Gk. *Eucharistia*, "thanksgiving"), with its "remembrance" of Christ's presence and its anticipation or expectation of the eschatological banquet with Christ's consummating coming (1 Cor. 11:24–26). This is the time of the church's mission to the nations (Mark 13:10); of Christ's presence in his Spirit (John 14:18–19; 16:14, 16); and of hope lived in anticipation of God's fulfillment of his creative purposes for the full range of God's creatures, awaiting that fulfillment, and suffering in that time of waiting (Rom. 8:18–25; 1 Cor. 1:7; Gal. 5:5; Jude 21; Phil. 3:10–14).

Perhaps, then, the diverse eschatological images in the Scriptures may be summarized by emphasizing the following points: the kingdom of God as manifested through assent to Jesus Christ's proclamation of the coming of God's lordly rule; the promise of God's faithfulness to creation as renewed in the raising of Jesus; and the anticipation of the consummation of all things in their acknowledgment of Jesus Christ. Christian hope, then, is Christ-centered. "The centuries-old hopes that have been projected into the future or into the present for so long have become real in Jesus. He is the realization of the future and therefore the goal of history."[7]

The Fourth Gospel

It is in the Fourth Gospel, the Gospel traditionally attributed to St. John, that these themes are most accentuated. This distinctive approach to eschatology, and in particular the imminence of God's consummating coming in Christ, takes shape in and through Jesus as the presence of God's creative and redemptive Word enfleshed (John 1:14). This theme is so pronounced in the Gospel that Ernst Käsemann, albeit with more than a little exaggeration, declares that "John changes the Galilean teacher into the God who goes about on earth."[8]

The theme of the kingdom of God is muted in the Fourth Gospel, appearing only rarely, and it is largely replaced by the image of *zōē ainōnios*, "eternal life" (see Dan. 12:2). The Synoptics do use terms such as "life" and "eternal life" (Matt. 19:16–17, 29; Mark 10:29–30; Luke 18:26), and these function as synonyms for the "kingdom of God" at various points (Matt. 19:23–29; Mark 9:43–47; 10:17–30; Luke 18:24–30). Yet, in the Fourth Gospel's interpretation and development of the phrase, its emphasis has shifted in two noticeable areas: from the kingdom that is *coming* to the life of divine

---

7. Schwarz, "Eschatology," 492.

8. Ernst Käsemann, *The Testament of Jesus: Study of the Gospel of John in the Light of Chapter 17*, trans. Gerhard Krodel (London: SCM, 1968), 27.

blessing that *has come*; and from the kingdom of *God* as manifested through the life and message of Jesus to the eternal life that following or having faith *in Jesus*, the definitive revelation of God, brings. The shifts are so evidently extensive that many scholars since David Strauss (1808–1874) have despaired of finding historical continuities between the Fourth Gospel and the earliest Christian proclamation.[9]

In Christ comes God's judgment (John 3:16–21, 36). In him comes the new life, as depicted eminently in the images of the new birth in the Spirit (3:3–9), the resurrection (14:6), life in Christ's life (14:19), the gift of the abiding Spirit (14:16–17; 20:22), the indwelling of the Father and Son (14:23), and the oneness of Christ's followers with him and each other (17:23) expressed in love (15:14–17). In Christ "self-judgment" is provoked as people "line up for or against him."[10] Believing in Christ is the only proper response to God's eschatological event in Christ (e.g., 3:16). Believers are assured that they have eternal life now (5:24), a life in Christ that is described as what God has in God's self (5:26). "Now claims to see God are regarded as claims to see Jesus. In John 1:14, we read of the tabernacling of the divine word in history not as an event in the future but as an event in the past, in the person of Jesus of Nazareth."[11]

Accordingly, "the future tenses normal in eschatological speech are constrained to become present tenses in order to make clear that the end of history is in fact being experienced in the midst of its course."[12] It is not insignificant, then, that "hope" is a term that does not appear in the Fourth Gospel. The emphasis falls instead on faith in, and love of, Christ. "The focus for attention for Christian life is the present. Since eternal life begins with believing in Jesus, in a sense hope is swallowed up by faith and love."[13]

John's Gospel certainly does not dispense with a futural element, as if all has been realized here and now in the mission and ministry of Jesus (e.g., John 5:28–29; 6:39). The Gospel suggests the *coming* of resurrected life

9. See Rudolf Bultmann, *Jesus and the Word*, trans. Louise Pettibone Smith and Erminie Huntress Lantero (London: Collins, 1958), 17.

10. Raymond E. Brown, *The Gospel according to John I–XI* (Garden City, NY: Doubleday, 1966), cxvii.

11. Rowland, "The Eschatology of the New Testament Church," 61. See John 14:7, 9.

12. C. K. Barrett, *The Gospel according to St John: An Introduction with Commentary and Notes on the Greek Text* (London: SPCK, 1956), 56.

13. Daniel J. Harrington, "The Future Is Now: Eternal Life and Hope in John's Gospel," in *Hope: Promise, Possibility, and Fulfillment*, ed. Richard Lennan and Nancy Pineda-Madrid (New York: Paulist, 2013), 192.

(6:39–40, 54); eternal life (12:25); judgment (5:28–29; 12:48); the *parousia* (14:3, 18, 28); and the tribulations inflicted on Christ's followers (chs. 15–16). The disciples anticipate a time when they will dwell in perfection in Christ and behold his glory (17:24). Yet the Gospel does put this futural dynamic into a perspective that enhances the quality of the eschatological life realized in Christ. So while John 5:28–29 speaks of the raising of the dead in "the hour" that "is coming," Jesus announces just before that that "hour is coming, and is now here" (5:25). When Martha expresses to Jesus her faith that her recently deceased brother, Lazarus, "will rise again in the resurrection on the last day," Jesus replies, "I am the resurrection and the life. Those who believe in me, even though they die, will live, and everyone who lives and believes in me will never die" (11:24–25).

Finally, and crucially, "The early Christians believed that the eschatological salvation was not wholly future, for the experience of the Spirit, such a dominant feature of early Christian religion, cannot be understood apart from the eschatological perspective."[14] In keeping with the intensified presence of God's eschatological renewing in Christ, this early Christian witness is accentuated in the Fourth Gospel. The promise of Jesus's return is preeminently located in the coming of Jesus in the Spirit (John 14:18–19; 16:14), the Spirit with whom the raised Jesus gifted the disciples (20:22). The presence of the Spirit involves the indwelling of believers by the Father and the Son. Accordingly, it is particularly through pneumatology that the Gospel of John can be seen as having "such a high regard for the possibilities of the present life of the Christian believer. . . . Because Johannine Christians valued so highly the presence of the Spirit in the experience of the Christian community, they could declare that the future blessings are already present."[15]

Irenaeus of Lyons (c. 130–c. 200)

According to G. W. H. Lampe, "The pace of doctrinal formulation was quickened during the second century by the clash of conflicting systems which derived their beliefs in part, at least, from outside the main Christian tradition represented by the New Testament writings." He continues: "Much of the advance in Christian self-understanding in the period which

14. Rowland, "The Eschatology of the New Testament Church," 58.
15. Robert Kysar, *John: The Maverick Gospel*, rev. ed. (Louisville: Westminster John Knox, 1995), 106.

separates the Apostolic Fathers from the theologians of the 3rd century was due to the need to examine and evaluate, and often refute and replace with a more satisfactory theology, the ideas propagated by a series of teachers, many of whom visited or settled in Rome, which became the most lively centre of debate."[16]

Irenaeus was involved in addressing some of the Roman developments to which Lampe refers. Arguably the most important theologian of the second century, the Greek-speaking bishop of Lyons occupies a crucial theological position between the immediate postapostolic period and that of the particularly theologically creative third century. He wrote, not only with a memory of recent imperial persecution of the Christian communities in Gaul, but also in the polemical fires of theological controversy. The most famous and important of his writings is his five-volume work *The Refutation and Overthrow of Knowledge Falsely So-Called* (better known by the short title *Against Heresies*). This work attempted to confute the teachings of various groups that, at least in some form, claimed to be "Christian." Apparently several Greek merchants in Irenaeus's diocese had begun an oratorial campaign praising the pursuit of *gnosis*.[17] Not only did many of these "Gnostic" groups appeal to Scripture for support, but they also drew on more esoteric and locally available "secret" traditions that were said to be derived from the apostles themselves. Irenaeus argued against these groups and in defense of the church's traditional teachings. "Not to exclude the heretics from the Church, Irenaeus argued, would damage its mission. Non-Christians would suppose they were representative of Christianity, and turn their ears away from the proclamation of the truth."[18]

Famously, Irenaeus responds to groups such as the Valentinians, Basilideans, and Marcionites by providing a series of rules to indicate why the

16. G. W. H. Lampe, "Christian Theology in the Patristic Period," in *A History of Christian Doctrine*, ed. Hubert Cunliffe-Jones (Edinburgh: T&T Clark, 1978), 28.

17. "Gnosticism" was largely rooted in pre-Christian Hellenistic religious cults and philosophies, possibly influenced by Persian mythologies. One must be careful with the term, however, since scholars have used it as an umbrella term for a wide variety of practices, religiosities, and systems of belief that are linked by their ontologically dualistic tendencies and their privileging of a *gnosis* (knowledge) for salvation. More recent scholarship, however, has observed that an emphasis on a soteriological gnosis in fact is not common among them. What is shared, instead, is their dualistic attitude toward creation. See M. A. Williams, *Rethinking "Gnosticism": An Argument for the Dismantling of a Dubious Category* (Princeton: Princeton University Press, 1999), 51-53.

18. Dennis Minns, *Irenaeus* (London: Geoffrey Chapman, 1994), 11, citing *Against Heresies* 1.25.3.

church's witness should be trusted as reliable and authoritative.[19] Of particular interest is the way he conceives of the eschatologically significant question of where God's healing presence may be found and of what it consists—the incarnate presence of God's Logos or Word.

For Irenaeus, the incarnation plays a very important role in Christian belief and practice. Even Irenaeus's theological appeal to authority is christological—Christ himself is the ground and basis of Christian belief and practice. He is the enfleshed manifestation of God's own revealing Word, the incarnated Son who is the very archetype of the image of God, and the one in whose image human beings are made. Irenaeus accordingly tends to articulate his account of the "image of God" through the lens of John 1:3 rather than Genesis 1. "The Son reveals the true human form through his incarnation, demonstrating at the same time that man is indeed in the image of God. . . . Thus the fashioning of the human flesh is intimately connected to Christ, the archetype of man, and his revelation of the image of God, the manifestation of both God and man."[20]

Not only is Christology the ground and grammar of Irenaeus's theology of creation and God's saving repair of it; Christology is inseparable from his use of eschatological imagery. Eschatology and incarnation cannot be disentangled, since Christology is, in a significant sense, concerned with an eschatological event. Behind Irenaeus's very lengthy and painstaking disputes with the heterodox groups on theological matters, that is, on the trustworthiness of the church's witness, and behind the various eschatological images Irenaeus provides, there lies a profound concern to do justice to the eschatological coming of God in Jesus Christ, the incarnate Word. So, Irenaeus argues, "the glory of God is the living man, and the life of man is the vision of God."[21] The significance of what God is *doing* eschatologically can never be understood until *who* God is for creatures in Christ is appreciated. To introduce a heterodox understanding of God and God's relation to the world is to undermine the very significance of God's saving act in Christ.

---

19. Whether in so doing he fairly and accurately portrays his opponents' views and cosmological concerns is questionable, but it is not relevant for the discussion in this book on Christian hope.

20. John Behr, *Asceticism and Anthropology in Irenaeus and Clement* (Oxford: Oxford University Press, 2000), 90.

21. Irenaeus, *Against Heresies* 4.20.7, in Robert M. Grant, *Irenaeus of Lyons* (London: Routledge, 1997), 116.

The Unassumed Is the Unhealed: Recapitulation

Two of the regulating rules in Irenaeus's theological account are the convictions summarized later by Gregory the Theologian: that only God can save, and that the unassumed is the unhealed (thus the Savior must be both divine and human).[22] As Irenaeus himself argued, "unless man had been joined to God, he could never have become a partaker of incorruptibility."[23]

The clue to what this involves can be found in his typological reading of all things in the *oikonomia* (economy) of God, expressed in his "most distinctive exposition" of the concept of "recapitulation."[24] In classical Greek, the word translated "recapitulation" derives from *kephalaion*, denoting the top of one's head or, in literature, a chapter. The word *anakephalaiōsis* is the act of making a summary of the chapters of a work, a resumé of its principal ideas, a compendium. It is used in Ephesians 1:10 to describe God's summing or gathering "up all things in him [Jesus Christ], things in heaven and things on earth." In Colossians 1:15-16 all things have been created in, through, and for the one who is the image of the invisible God. Irenaeus unites these themes with the Pauline idea of Christ as "the head over all things," referring to Christ as the one in whom all things find their unity, as their origin (as the creative agency of God and the archetypal image) and their end (who sums all things up, and raises them to participate in God's eternal life). Thus Christ, for Irenaeus, takes up and summarizes all creatures in himself.[25]

However, the most immediate reference is that of the Adam-Christ typology (Rom. 5:12-21). Albeit far removed from the divine perfection and incorruptibility, because of the infinite distance separating him from God, Adam had enjoyed a supernatural endowment through the action of the Spirit in Paradise. God's intention was to allow weak and childlike Adam to advance freely toward ever-closer resemblance to, and perfect relationship with, his Maker. However, through his disobedience Adam lost the "image and likeness" of God and fell into bondage to the devil. For Irenaeus, whatever Adam's reasons for disobedience, his actions had serious consequences

22. Gregory of Nazianzus, *Epistle* 101.7.

23. Irenaeus, *Against Heresies* 3.18.7, in *Ante-Nicene Fathers*, ed. Philip Schaff, vol. 1 (repr. ʼʁ͏ͱͳͳͳ ͏ͱͰͱͰͱͰ ͏ͱͱͱͱͱͱ ͱͰ ͱͱͱ), ͱ ͱ ͱ

24. John Lawson, *The Biblical Theology of St. Irenaeus of Lyons* (London. Epworth, 1948), 140.

25. Trevor A. Hart, "Irenaeus, Recapitulation, and Physical Redemption," in *Christ in Our Place: The Humanity of God in Christ for the Reconciliation of the World*, ed. Trevor Hart and Daniel P. Thimell (Exeter: Paternoster, 1989), 175.

for all his descendants. His sin was the source of all sin and mortality, so that *all* of humanity has become enslaved to the devil, has lost life, and suffers corruption and death. Humanity, separating itself from God, has become savage, murderous, and avaricious in its affairs, to the point of considering its own kin as enemies to be killed.

Christ is the New Man who arrives in the last times to fulfill God's purposes for human beings. It is important not to mistake Irenaeus's claim here as a way of asserting that human beings, without Christ's renewing, organically and developmentally progress toward human perfection. Christ's is a recapitulatory performance, not only in that it sums up all things, and can do so since he is God's own creative Word through whom all things come to be; rather, it is saving precisely because it radically reverses the trajectory and destructive significance of Adam's sin. Humanity's disobedience is undone by Christ's obedience, its corruption by his incorruption, its falling into death by his life, its sinfulness by his communion with God, its animosity toward God by his restoration of friendship with God, and so on. This is a "conception of 'going over the ground again', . . . but with the opposite result."[26]

> In victorious conflict with Satan, and his fulfilment of the righteous will of his Father, Christ remoulds human nature and establishes it on a new footing before God, "through obedience doing away with disobedience completely", since "as by the disobedience of the one man who was originally moulded from virgin soil, the many were made sinners, and forfeited life; so was it necessary that, by the obedience of the one man, who was originally born from a virgin, many should be justified and receive salvation."[27]

This Pauline Adam-Christ parallel affirms that Christ was himself "the first of the living, because Adam had become the first of the dead."[28] In his gathering together and summing up all things in himself, Christ becomes the firstfruits of the new humanity, pouring out upon human beings that paternal grace that belongs by nature to him alone in his relationship with the Father, drawing restored humanity into conformity to his likeness and into fellowship with God.

---

26. Lawson, *The Biblical Theology of St. Irenaeus of Lyons*, 143.

27. Hart, "Irenaeus, Recapitulation, and Physical Redemption," 172, citing *Against Heresies* 2.18.6; 3.18.7.

28. *Against Heresies* 3.22.4, in Grant, *Irenaeus of Lyons*, 106.

An Eschatology of the Healed Creature

The eschatological significance of these claims of being graciously conformed into the likeness of God in the Son and by the Spirit is substantial. "The human creation in the image and likeness of God is directly tied to the *telos* [end or purpose] of the ultimate *visio dei* [vision of God]. . . . God, as it were, continues his creative activity which he had started in Paradise, and which will ultimately lead to the vision of God."[29] Accordingly, the vision of God is the ultimate purpose of the ways of God with and for the world.

Irenaeus provides a stringently "holistic" approach to the eschatological vision of God. In contrast to the ontological dualism that is inherent in the notion that salvation is a liberation of the "spiritual" person from material bondage through knowledge of one's heavenly origin, Irenaeus offers a series of arguments closely tying God's actions to an *embodied* healing. Not only can there be no schism between the Creator of the world and the God of Jesus Christ but, on the contrary, the creative God is the one who creates all things from God's goodness in and through the Word. Human beings are created as physical and not merely rational souls. The creative God "perfects" the creature, "in accordance with the image and likeness of God," "and makes us fit for life" in the Word.[30] The incarnate Word is he who "because of his immeasurable love became what we are in order to make us what he is."[31]

The eschatological implications of sin are preeminently presented in terms of corruption, mortality, and death. Accordingly, the event of God's incarnate coming in Christ communicates the divine condition of incorruption and immortality. Hence, although Irenaeus avoids the term *theopoiēsis* (deification), he does at least speak of humanity as passing "into God" and of "promotion into God" in the redemptive process.[32] So, he asserts, the heretics who take Paul's claim that flesh and blood cannot enter the kingdom of God (1 Cor. 15:50), and from that spiritualize life, have entirely misunderstood the mind of the apostle and thereby overturn the whole *oikonomia* (economy) of God. This Pauline verse is speaking of the "carnal actions" that lead to sin. After all, the Eucharist is an assurance of hope, hope for the resurrection of the body, and baptism is the seal of eternal life. "How can they

29. Hans Boersma, "Accommodation to What? University of Being Pure Nature, and the Anthropology of St. Irenaeus," *International Journal of Systematic Theology* 8, no. 3 (2006). 291.

30. *Against Heresies* 5.16.1, in Schaff, *Ante-Nicene Fathers*, 1:788.

31. *Against Heresies* 5.proem, in Grant, *Irenaeus of Lyons*, 123.

32. *Against Heresies* 3.33.4, in Schaff, *Ante-Nicene Fathers*, 1:734; 3.19.1, in Schaff, *Ante-Nicene Fathers*, 1:645.

say that the flesh goes to corruption and does not participate in life, when it is nourished by the Lord's body and his blood? . . . [S]o also our bodies which partake of the eucharist are no longer corruptible but have the hope of resurrection for ever."[33]

Irenaeus uses imagery that has a chiliastic quality about it, and he offers eschatological assertions that sit somewhat uncomfortably with his distinctively christological approach to creation and recapitulation. He occasionally even speculates about the post-death state in a way that undermines his otherwise focused reflections on the Scriptures. Without explanation or reason, he combines texts from the books of Daniel, Matthew, and Revelation. This literal-historical reading of the apocalyptic material seemingly became such an embarrassment to later readers that most medieval manuscripts of his *Against Heresies* do not even contain the final chapters of book 5. In these chapters he discusses the coming of the tribulation and the devastating work of the Antichrist, the resurrection of the just, the following thousand-year reign of Christ with its progressive realization of the likeness of God,[34] the final judgment, and the eternal kingdom of God in which the eternal Jerusalem will descend to the earth. The world will come to an end in as many millennia as the days in which Genesis 1 claims it was made—in other words, in the six thousandth year of its existence. Nonetheless, he does at least attempt to curb one form of speculation: that of attempting to work out the name of the Antichrist from the number of the beast in Revelation. Not only have the Scriptures not revealed a name, but the results of the search are varied, and consequently any miscalculation will actually end up with a failure to recognize the Antichrist when he appears. Irenaeus's appeal to traditional and biblical imagery of the Antichrist here "is a powerful antidote to any optimistic theory of the perfectability of the present order apart from a decisive act of God."[35]

Elements suggesting something like an intermediate state appear in Irenaeus's writing. The soul descends, like Christ, to an intermediate state (Hades) to await the resurrection of the body. This is contrary to the Gnostics' belief that a disembodied soul is taken to heaven at death. While on the one hand Irenaeus's suggestion may seem to be a theologically illegitimate

---

33. *Against Heresies* 4.18.5, in Schaff, *Ante-Nicene Fathers*, 1:701–2.

34. Christopher R. Smith claims that Irenaeus nowhere indicates that Christ's earthly kingdom will be a thousand years long. Smith, "Chiliasm and Recapitulation in the Theology of Irenaeus," *Vigiliae Christianae* 48 (1994): 315–18. Instead, the period is indeterminately long.

35. G. W. H. Lampe, "Early Patristic Eschatology," *Eschatology*, Scottish Journal of Theology Occasional Papers No. 2 (1953), 29.

move, a speculation and esoteric claim to know the future, on the other hand his notion does play an important theological role against Gnosticism. He rejects the idea that at the end of this earthly life the immortal soul immediately ascends to its heavenly abode, and he does so precisely in order to affirm the resurrection of the whole person (not merely the soul). Consequently, he describes the resurrection in very earthly terms, as the resurrection of the *flesh*. This approach prevents allegorical approaches to the material, out of concern not to undo the connection between God and the materiality of God's redemptive purposes, which culminate in the raising of the embodied person from death. In many ways, "Irenaeus' teaching on the last times is not, therefore, an aberrant appendage to his work, but shows him to be 'a consistent creationist.'"[36]

Divine justice necessitates that both the just and the unjust be raised bodily in order to receive their just deserts. Irenaeus holds to the traditional cycle of curse and blessing, the fulfillment of the judgment of divine justice over the self-condemned or unbelievers, judgment they have brought upon themselves as the result of their own choosing. The blessings entail that everything has been made subject to the lordship of Christ, who subjects himself to the Father so that God is all in all; and the reward of the just is communion with God.

Athanasius of Alexandria (c. 299–373)

For Irenaeus, all hope is radically christocentric, rooted in the image of God who is the Word and who becomes incarnate for creatures' perfection and renewal. It is an approach to God's saving act that reads back into the very act of creation itself. God's eschatological purposes are realized in and through the life of the incarnate Word. A good many of the themes present in Irenaeus reappear in Athanasius's work, though with different contexts and emphases.

Irenaeus, the bishop of Lyons, wrote in the second century to expose the anti-materialism of his opponents by emphasizing the place of materiality in the unified work of creation, recapitulation, and transforming resurrection. Athanasius, the highly influential bishop of Alexandria, on the other

---

36. John Behr, *Irenaeus of Lyons: Identifying Christianity*, Christian Theology in Context (Oxford: Oxford University Press, 2013), 181, citing Smith, "Chiliasm and Recapitulation in the Theology of Irenaeus," 320.

hand, wrote to expose the ontological subordinationism (that the Father is superior *in being* to the Son) of the presbyter Arius, who was accused of reducing the *Logos* (Word) of God to a *ktisma* (creature), the first of God's creative works, and therefore separating the Logos from the transcendent Father in the same way the creature is ontologically separated from God. Accordingly, Athanasius's interest is emphatically in defending the full deity of God's Logos, as a deity of the same ontological order as the Father. There is nothing that God is or has *as God* that the Logos or eternal Son does not share. In fact, the Son or Word of God is the fullness of God's very image, and it is through him that human beings are created in the image of God. This grounds a theological account of the unique stature and value of the created order as it participates in, and reflects, the oneness of the Son with the Father. Nonetheless, the theological overlaps between the two thinkers are notable: God creates through the Word, the image of God; the fall is into corruption and perishability; and the eschatologically saving event is described as "deification" (*theopoiēsis*).

For Athanasius as much as for Irenaeus, God created and willed humanity to live incorruptibly, and indeed immortally, knowing God and thereby living "the happy and truly blessed life" in a harmonious order.[37] But humanity lost that unending, blessed life through the fall, which brought the disruptive corruption of death and nothingness or "non-being through corruption," the dehumanizing undoing of God's creation (*DI* 63). "When then people turn from God, they renounce their proper role in the divine order and begin to cease to be what they were created to be."[38] God's action in Christ, the fully divine and human Word of God, is restorative: the Word re-creates human nature in his own life. That means that God's act is one of renewal, standing therefore in continuity with God's creative purposes (*DI* 7.5). "Like Irenaeus, Athanasius sees salvation in terms of a reorientation of fallen humanity towards the divine."[39] Athanasius justifies this in an account of what is *fitting* according to his understanding of the nature of the God who purposes creation for communion (*DI* 10). Therefore he insists on the saving *divine necessity*, that it is "improper" for God to let the creature "come into being to be neglected and destroyed" (*DI* 6). That means that once God "made him and created him out of nothing, it was most absurd that his

---

37. Athanasius, *On the Incarnation* (*De Incarnatione*), trans. John Behr (Yonkers, NY: St. Vladimir's Seminary Press, 2011), 75. Hereafter *DI*.

38. Alvyn Pettersen, *Athanasius* (London: Geoffrey Chapman, 1995), 85.

39. Norman Russell, *The Doctrine of Deification in the Greek Patristic Tradition* (Oxford: Oxford University Press, 2004), 169.

works should be destroyed, and especially before the sight of the maker. It was therefore right not to permit human beings to be carried away by corruption, because this would be improper to and unworthy of the goodness of God" (*DI* 6).

But God's work is more than simply restorative; it is eschatological. "In creation and redemption, God does one thing" with the giving and receiving of divine love.[40] Redemption is not only rescue, a return to one's original state; it is also eschatological cure. "We are not only redeemed from something, we are also redeemed into something."[41] In fact, Athanasius's account of creation is already eschatologically significant, given the immortal life into which God calls mortal and mutable creatures through participation in the creative Word, the image of God. So "creation as it comes from the mouth of God at the beginning is not yet fulfilled. It is created mobile and mutable, and thus designed to move from glory to glory. . . . [C]reation has a built-in eschatology."[42]

The assumption of flesh by the eternal Word of God communicates the sheer divine gift of God's own life to humanity. In this way Athanasius offers more than simply a claim that the Son brings new life, redeeming corruptibility and mortality and making the new creation. In a letter to Serapion, Athanasius declares that all things receive the characteristics of that in which they participate, and it is this sense of *participation* and of *solidarity* of the whole human race that drives his eschatology. To put it most acutely, Athanasius offers an eschatology of the divine presence in and with creatures that is the condition for the creatures' presence with God. The Word's dwelling among us was in order to redeem, sanctify, and deify the human race. By participating in the Spirit of Christ we become holy; by participating in the Word we are able to contemplate the Father. Pointing to Christ's humbling himself in order to exalt human beings, Athanasius claims, "He was incarnate that we might be made god; and he manifested himself through a body that we might receive an idea of the invisible Father" (*DI* 54). Rarely does he use the term "gods" of human beings when speaking theologically, but when he does his sense is clear. To Serapion he declares that if some have been called gods, then this refers not to their nature but to their participation in the Son. It is this perspective that enables Athanasius to offer a soteriologically

40. Rowan Williams, "Athanasius and the Arian Crisis," in *The First Christian Theologians: An Introduction to Theology in the Early Church*, ed. G. R. Evans (Malden: Blackwell, 2004), 164.

41. H. E. W. Turner, *The Patristic Doctrine of Redemption* (London: A. R. Mowbray, 1952), 117.

42. Peter J. Leithart, *Athanasius* (Grand Rapids: Baker Academic, 2011), 97.

driven, anti-Arian argument in which the deifying power of the Son and of the Spirit is both taken for granted and used as an argument to demonstrate their full divinity. If the Son and the Spirit are not very God of very God, then we cannot be deified; rather, we would be united with a creature.

Athanasius is clear what "deification" is and is not. First, in this participation or deification, the Son himself is unmistakably set apart as participated in rather than as a participant. He is divine by nature, and his flesh participates in that deity necessarily.[43] Second, the participation of human beings in the Son's deifying grace is a gift and is not based on any likeness achieved from the human side. Third, it is not a claim that human beings become something other than what they are. On the contrary, they become what they were created to be, creatures who participate in God's own life. "Deification is about proper use of flesh, not about the destruction of flesh."[44] For this reason Athanasius objects that the senate has no authority to deify when its members are merely human: those who make gods should be gods themselves. Fourth, deification does not mean that the ethical life is unnecessary. Some scholars regard Athanasius as having underplayed virtue and creaturely agency in his writing,[45] but it is clear enough that human beings are to live the lives they have been created for, in obedience to God. Fifth, and finally, deification is not a sharing in the essence of God, but rather a relationship to God rooted in the communion with God's Son and Spirit. The prominence of filial categories is everywhere evident. Accordingly, "deification" is interchangeable with terms such as "adoption, renewal, salvation, sanctification, grace, transcendence, illumination, and vivification."[46] The Spirit is the Son's Spirit of adoption.[47]

Irenaeus and Athanasius focus on a number of common themes, but Irenaeus's millenarianism dissipates in Athanasius's writings. And it does so without any detriment to belief in the resurrection *of the body* in Christ and the materiality of the life everlasting. Athanasius uses the concept of deification in a holistic manner. The sense of this partly derives from his treatment of the incarnation, the redeeming flesh that the Logos assumed and thereby deified. The Logos deified that which he put on; he made the body immortal;

43. Athanasius, *Against the Arians* 1.39, in Khaled Anatolios, *Athanasius* (London: Routledge, 2004), 78.

44. Leithart, *Athanasius*, 160.

45. J. N. D. Kelly, *Early Christian Doctrines*, 5th ed. (London: A&C Black, 1977), 184, 379; Frances Young, *From Nicaea to Chalcedon: A Guide to the Literature and Its Background* (London: SCM, 1983), 185; Russell, *The Doctrine of Deification*, 188.

46. Russell, *The Doctrine of Deification*, 177.

47. Athanasius, *Letter to Serapion on the Holy Spirit* 1.25, in Anatolios, *Athanasius*, 182.

he renewed and exalted human nature; and in his resurrection he raised it. Now the flesh has arisen from its mortality and has been deified. Athanasius rarely offers images of what that new life looks like, but in one place he draws eschatologically on the image of the peaceableness of God from Isaiah 2:4.

Karl Barth (1886–1968)

Jesus Christ Our Hope

Because of Karl Barth's deteriorating health, the composition of his *Church Dogmatics* was brought to an abrupt end prior to its planned completion with the eschatologically themed fifth volume. Barth himself remarked, "There is a certain merit to an unfinished dogmatics; it points to the eschatological nature of theology."[48] This importantly implies that eschatology is not an isolatable aspect within, or at the end of, a dogmatic system, but pervades dogmatic work.

What is Christian hope for Barth? Such a question would be more than a little odd to Barth, since it asks about *things* hoped for. Eschatology cannot be the study of the *eschata* (the "last things") as such, but rather has to do with the *eschatos*, he who is our End. As Karl Rahner importantly argues, "*Christ* himself is the hermeneutical principle of all eschatological assertions. Anything that cannot be read and understood as a christological assertion is not a genuine eschatological assertion."[49] Barth was engaged in defining and applying such a theological hermeneutic from the mid-1920s in Göttingen. Jesus Christ is the way God reveals God's self; Jesus Christ is he in whom God reveals God's self; and God's self-revealedness is the Spirit's witness to this Christ. Jesus Christ is the way God is toward us, and God's ways are always in and through this one. This culminates in Barth's treatment of Jesus Christ as "electing God" and "elect man." Christ is the creative, elective agency of God, and he is himself the one acted through and on. Not only, then, is there no absconded God hiding in the world's unseen hindparts or even shadows, but there can be no human abstracted or absconded from its *christic* being-in-covenantal-performance. "God and man" and their en-

48. Karl Barth, quoted in John D. Godsey, "Barth as Teacher," in *For the Sake of the World: Karl Barth and the Future of Ecclesial Theology*, ed. George Hunsinger (Grand Rapids: Eerdmans, 2004), 214.

49. Karl Rahner, "The Hermeneutics of Eschatological Assertions," in *Theological Investigations*, 23 vols. (London: Darton, Longman and Todd, 1961–1992), 4:342–43.

counter "are not for us unwritten pages or unknown quantities."[50] All things have their being in God's gracious eternal decision, and no one or no thing has its being outside or independent of this decision. In fact, there can be no abstract way of understanding terms such as "time" and "eternity," no way that does not reflect the reality of God's decision in Jesus Christ. Consequently, "we have to say that eternity bears the name Jesus Christ"; Jesus Christ is real, eschatological time.[51]

Barth, in other words, came to ask the question "for what may we hope?" christologically. Or, better, he came to ask "for whom may we hope?", and therefore sought to ground and regulate the talk of hope that is proper to Christians in Jesus Christ. "The New Testament does not hope for the attainment merely of abstract blessings. . . . Strictly speaking, there are no 'last things', i.e., no abstract and autonomous last things apart from and alongside Him [Jesus Christ], the last One" (*CD* III/2, 490). Likewise, Christ, then, as the incarnate coming of God, is not a mere "means or instrument or channel," "some general gift"; on the contrary, he is "the One in whom the Christian is summoned to hope" (*CD* IV/1, 116). Eschatology is about Jesus Christ in three forms of his effective presence, or his threefold *parousia*: resurrected life, presence in the Spirit, and consummating coming. Among other things, this means that the Spirit is not a compensation for an essentially *absent* Christ, but rather is the form of the presence of the ascended Christ, God's own self. Moreover, it means that the consummating *parousia* will therefore not involve something different from the promised gracious presence of God in Christ. "God's kingdom is God himself . . . as he not merely is somewhere and somehow . . . but as he comes" (*CL*, 236). Consequently, "He who comes is the same as He who was and who is. . . . Nothing which will be has not already taken place on Easter Day—included and anticipated in the person of the one man Jesus" (*CD* III/2, 489).

We have hope in Christ's resurrection, and we hope for God in Christ's coming. That is why Barth emphasizes that "Jesus Christ is our hope."[52] In his obedient life and death, Jesus fulfilled that which humanity had not done, the covenant fellowship ("you will be my people") with the electing God ("I will be your God"). As the true human being (and true God), indeed the

50. Karl Barth, *The Christian Life: Church Dogmatics IV.4, Lecture Fragments*, trans. G. W. Bromiley (Edinburgh: T&T Clark, 2004), 5. Hereafter *CL*.

51. Karl Barth, *Church Dogmatics*, 14 vols. (Edinburgh: T&T Clark, 1956–1975), II/1, 622. Hereafter *CD*.

52. Karl Barth, *Credo: A Presentation of the Chief Problems of Dogmatics with Reference to the Apostles' Creed*, trans. James Strathern McNab (London: Hodder & Stoughton, 1936), 120.

prototypical human being, Christ is the eschatological one raised to eschatological/new life for the world. It is on this basis that Christian faith, love, and hope spring and take shape. Hence Barth argues that hope's "final and decisive basis lies in the fact that the prophetic action of Jesus Christ, and therefore . . . the kingdom of God come and the will of God done in Him, . . . while it is complete in itself, is only moving towards its fulfilment, i.e., not to an amplification or transcending of its content or declaration . . . but to a supremely radical alteration and extension of the mode and manner and form of its occurrence" (CD IV.3, 903).

These statements highlight a certain puzzle in understanding Barth. If everything is finished, then has he not prematurely foreclosed the future and undermined the time after Jesus's resurrection, "our time"? Is this not what Barth means when speaking, for example, of Christ's consummating coming as the "unveiling"/"revelation" of that which has been accomplished?[53] Yet that which is "complete in itself," in Christ's person, is "only moving towards its fulfilment," which, for us, is our "supremely radical alteration" in Christ. This time of eschatological provisionality—the "not yet" in us that moves from Christ's "already"—is what characterizes Barth's discourse on the "prophetic work" of Christ in Church Dogmatics IV/3, and his emphasis on mission. So, for now, we inhabit "the problematic present between the times" (CL, 172), "the interim period . . . the time given for the conversion of the world" (CD III/2, 489). It is in this time that hope is generated, is shaped by the resurrection event, is sustained by Christ's contemporary presence in the Spirit (pneumatological contemporaneity), and moves toward his consummating coming. Thus the Spirit is not a compensation for an absent Christ but the way in which the ascended Christ is made present. Despite the continued presence of sin and suffering, which still have to be driven from the field, hope receives a confidence appropriate to the belief that sin will be defeated by the risen Christ. Hope is for the "still awaited redemption of the world reconciled in Him."

In this context, Barth speaks of the future of all things in Christ being "open," but in a qualified way. It is not open in the sense of being neutral or indeterminate, a nothingness waiting to be filled by human acts. Barth rather speaks of the "most striking determination of time" in Christ (CD IV/3.1, 913) because it is God's gift of grace, the coming kingdom of God

---

53. For the details of the charge, and responses from Barth's *oeuvre*, see John C. McDowell, *Hope in Barth's Eschatology: Interrogations and Transformations beyond Tragedy* (Aldershot: Ashgate, 2000).

encounters the world as something entirely *new*. The kingdom of God is a "wholly new order, quite independent of all creaturely and even Christian development" (*CD* III/2, 486). Yet Christian hope cannot be ambivalent or hesitant about this future—expecting not twilight or shadow but "good and salvation" and the judgment of grace, since "the Subject of expectation, i.e., the One expected," is not a human projection (*CD* IV/3.2, 908). Hope is required for the consummation of all things, with Christ himself alone being "*the* rejected," taking the rejected person's place (*CD* II/2, 353).

Nonetheless, Barth is reticent to admit an eschatological universalism. Barth explicitly rejects the *apokatastasis* as presumptuous, on two main grounds. First, it is based on the conjunction of an optimistic estimate of humanity with the idea of the infinite potentiality of the divine being (*CD* II/2, 295). Second, it imposes a "right or necessity," or a metaphysical system, on God's election and calling (*CD* II/2, 417). We should add a third point: Barth refuses to speculate as to the exact form of the future. The nature of eschatological language is not to make assertions about what has not yet happened *in nobis* (in us), but to witness to the reality that has been accomplished in Christ. If Barth maintains a *hope* that the circle of election and calling will be finally and comprehensively enlarged, it is because he believes in the superabundant divine love and grace expressed in Christ. "One thing is sure, that there is no theological justification for setting any limits on our side to the friendliness of God towards man which appeared in Jesus Christ."[54]

Christ, then, is the world's universal and absolute future. It is to him that biblical images of eternal life, kingdom of God, etc., refer, and not to confident assertions about the shape of future history. Barth thereby rejects self-grounded hopes as illusions based in, for example, desires or needs, or hope for divine blessing on our activities as such. Moreover, Christian hope disrupts thoughts of the simple continuity of life through death, as expressed in doctrines of the soul's immortality, and the belief that our agency can or "must laboriously build the road to" the future.[55]

---

54. Karl Barth, "The Humanity of God," in *God, Grace and Gospel* (Edinburgh: Oliver & Boyd, 1959), 50.

55. Karl Barth, *Dogmatics in Outline*, trans. G. T. Thomson (London: SCM, 1949), 133.

Hope's Strange Kind of Waiting: Acting in Hope

Karl Marx (1818–1883) recognized hope's regulative function. His hope for the communist society played an important part in determining the nature of his critique of modern capitalist societies, and he had noted how Christian belief/hope operates in redirecting the vision of those alienated from the products of their labor, each other, and themselves.

Mentioning Marx here is highly appropriate when it is remembered that Barth, when pastor in Safenwil (1911–1921), became actively involved in the social and political affairs of his parish, even joining for a time the Social Democratic Party. Barth the "red pastor" crusading for justice was to mature into the theologian of freedom—divine freedom and its mirroring in social, political, and personal affairs. As a consequence of these practical engagements and his developing theological perspective, Barth believed that Christian hope cannot legitimately be that which Marx and others claimed it to be—a shying away from the practical processes of engaging with the world's injustices. Eschatology, and the fragile hope that it inspires (fragile because it is a human act in response to grace), cannot be motivated by idle curiosity or speculative knowledge. "Hope in [Jesus Christ] is not an inactive hope" (CD IV/4, 209). Therefore, one must refuse to dislocate hope and human agency, souls and bodies, the individual and the community, and instead must positively depict hope as activating that agency in, among other things, a "zeal for the honor of God," with its corresponding "struggle for human righteousness" and "revolt against disorder" (CL, 111, 205). In applying these themes to a non-escapist ethic, Barth claims that the hope for Christ's coming (for God's being all in all, redemption of the world in Christ, and sin's destruction) necessarily determines the shape of hope's active expression in "our whole life."[56]

Eschatology, then, "the rude incursion of God's kingdom" in Christ, provides an image (or rather a "Reality") that shows interim time to be corrupted by sin, yet also the context created, sustained, and reconciled by God's love in Christ. Hope seeks to liberate humanity from all things that dehumanize it, to act against needless suffering, and to participate in God's "de-demonizing" of the world, while still realizing that guidelines for human acting depend on actual concrete circumstances. This responsible action of Christian witness is "kingdom-like," a "modest but clear analogue" to, a parable of, and witness to God's action in Christ (CL, 26, 175).

56. Barth, Dogmatics in Outline, 154.

Conclusion

This book has introduced four broad ways of reading eschatological statements regarding the content of Christian hope. They summarize broad trends in understanding what those eschatological statements are and do: the apocalyptic, existential, political, and christological. One should, of course, exercise caution when using them even in this way, lest they be construed as discrete and exclusive (there are overlaps between them) or as simple and coherent categories (there are multiple types of approaches even within each). Through the use of these categories, we have indicated the richness of the traditions of Christian hope and have outlined the marked differences between writers who might otherwise appear to be saying broadly similar things about that hope.

Perspectives on Christian hope cannot be isolated from other doctrinal commitments. All Christian doctrines depend on other Christian doctrines, and shifts in one have implications for others. Claims about the nature and shape of hope are informed by claims about how God, creation, sin and reconciliation, and so on, are all to be conceived. (Of course, this means that these doctrines are concomitantly bound up with eschatology. "Apart from hope in God, every Christian doctrine becomes distorted.")[1] It should also be clear that, while images of resurrection, last judgment, and eternal life and reprobation were fairly standard throughout the Christian tradition, different thinkers have highlighted different images concerning the so-called last things according to the theological framework or proj-

---

1. Daniel L. Migliore, *Faith Seeking Understanding: An Introduction to Christian Theology*, 3rd ed. (Grand Rapids: Eerdmans, 2014), 347.

ect or interpretive keys they are working with: for example, Irenaeus emphasizes the physical millennium and the materiality of the resurrection body; Athanasius underlines the incorruption that the immortal God gives; Bultmann privileges the encounter with God in the moment of faith's decision; and Moltmann stresses the coming reconciliation in the indwelling or *shekinah* of God.[2]

Numerous issues should be kept in mind in approaching Christian hope today. First, as the above suggests, one has to acknowledge the multiplicity of approaches and to understand what conditions and animates them.

Second, one should recognize that there is a gap between individual and corporate concerns. The Enlightenment accentuated the individualistic strains in the Christian traditions, and in so doing it pressed home a separation of body and soul, such as can be seen in the anthropological dualism of René Descartes (1596–1650). This takes shape, eschatologically speaking, in a stress on the immortality of the soul, such as we find in Immanuel Kant (1724–1804). Kant postulated that an immortal state is required in order to perfect the moral agent. While few theologians have followed this reasoning on the immortality of the soul in any straightforward way, these early modern conceptual developments exacerbated the trends within some accounts of Christian hope to individualize and spiritualize that hope. This occurs in the nineteenth-century liberal Protestant theological tradition represented by Adolf von Harnack, for whom the kingdom of God is God's reign in the human heart. But it is also reflected in theologies that in other ways appear more traditional, or in continuity with the dominant strands of the Christian tradition. As one commentator lamented some years ago, "The popular evangelical instinct is to move quickly to the question of salvation, put crudely, to want to know who gets saved, or who goes to heaven." He complains that "this represents a preoccupation with sin, to the detriment of the doctrine of creation," restricts "the work of the Spirit to the application of salvation within the Church," loses "sight . . . of the all-encompassing presence of the Spirit within the world," and reduces salvation to "removal from world to 'heaven', rather than the return of all things to the creator in order that God may be glorified in them." Accordingly, "the scope of God's and the Church's mission is reduced in this way to preparing souls for heaven

---

2. It is worth pointing out that, logically speaking, images such as the earthly millennium, the intermediate state and purgatory, even resurrection and the last judgment, are not technically *last things* but rather penultimate ones. In other words, they provide the conditions for the eternal communion with God or the damnation of the reprobate.

rather than serving the divine purpose of the restoration of all things."[3] Can we be human without others? And can we and others be human without our bodies? If nothing else, the individualistic interpretations of hope speak of the integrity of each person and of the need to refuse to reduce persons to their bodily desires.

Third, and following from this, the differences between predominantly spiritualistic and more holistic hopes have tremendous implications for this world. In certain apocalyptic schemes, there is little hope for this world, and the overwhelming emphasis is on the world's destruction and the believer's escape from it. Heaven is then construed as a replacement, a new world, rather than this world made new or renewed. In marked contrast, the mood of Harnack's theology is overwhelmingly one of continuity between that which is and that which is to come. H. Richard Niebuhr sarcastically commented on this tradition and its impact on American theologians: "A God without wrath brought men without sin into a kingdom without judgment through the ministry of a Christ without a cross."[4] Yet the images of the resurrection of the body, the new creation, the new Jerusalem, and the new heavens and the new earth are deeply earthy and holistic images, and they suggest that the Christian tradition has largely maintained a position somewhere in between discontinuity and continuity by articulating the divine transformation and consummation of all things. "The New Testament witnesses envision a consummation of the world which is not primarily destruction. It is rather the universal incorporation into the creative and transforming act of Christ's resurrection."[5] In fact, it entails a cosmic reconciliation that includes the nonhuman creature, as God's work of creation is eschatologically perfected and God's creative purposes are fulfilled (e.g., Rom. 8:21). That perspective entails that "the kingdom of God is the perfect realization of the destiny of human persons for a life in perfect communion among themselves" through communion with God.[6] As such, the "communal life is conditioned by peace and justice, because the disruption of peace destroys the community." A powerful element within the Christian traditions has stressed the continuity of the church and the kingdom of God, though

---

3. Nigel Wright, *The Radical Evangelical: Seeking a Place to Stand* (London: SPCK, 1996), 37.

4. H. Richard Niebuhr, *The Kingdom of God in America* (New York: Harper Torchbooks, 1959), 193.

5. Hans Schwarz, *Eschatology* (Grand Rapids: Eerdmans, 2000), 389.

6. Wolfhart Pannenberg, "The Task of Christian Eschatology," in *The Last Things: Biblical and Theological Perspectives on Eschatology*, ed. Carl E. Braaten and Robert W. Jenson (Grand Rapids: Eerdmans, 2002), 5.

many have asserted the need for a process of transformation before the life of perfect communion can begin.[7]

The fourth issue is closely related. If Christians are to hope for the fulfillment of God's redemptive work in renewing all things, how are we to understand the image of the last judgment as involving an act of separation, and therefore an eternal perdition or reprobation? At the least, God's love and God's wrath should not be opposed to one another, even if certain forms of apocalypticism want to mete out divine vengeance against those identified as wicked. Therefore, "it will not do to portray God as fundamentally loving until we reach the point of discussing the nature of hell, and suddenly portray God as fundamentally a just God."[8] God's love and God's wrath cannot be conceptually set alongside each other as separate and successive moments within the life of God turned toward God's creatures; nor can they be construed as conflicting divine character traits. Marcion suggested something like this in the mid-second century and accordingly argued that the vengeful God of the Old Testament was, in fact, an entirely different and inferior God, a *demiurge*, from the Father of Jesus Christ. Yet, here, and in many other areas, Marcion's example was not followed by the bulk of the Christian traditions. After all, "the Bible gives us no warrant for isolating God's love and justice in this fashion."[9] Rather, wrath can be conceived of as the underside of the love of the self-consistent or simple God, an expression of that love against all that diminishes, distorts, disrupts, and perverts the goodness of the product of God's creative action. As a consequence, God's wrath is not temporary. It perseveres against wickedness or sin, and it uncovers the nature and implications of creaturely sin. In Revelation, it is even predicated of the lamb that was slain (Rev. 6:16).

The crucial question, however, remains: What does it mean to confess a "comprehensive vision of the transformation of all things in the light of

7. By the thirteenth century it was common for these traditions to require a postmortem preparatory and purgatorial state, a state of purification (*purgatorium*) that was poetically depicted by Dante. "Purgatory's inhabitants . . . are in heaven's antechamber . . . preparing for eternal, loving intimacy with God." Paul J. Griffiths, "Purgatory," in *The Oxford Handbook of Eschatology*, ed. Jerry L. Walls (Oxford: Oxford University Press, 2008), 427. According to Joseph Ratzinger, purgatory involves "the inwardly necessary process of transformation in which a person becomes capable of Christ, capable of God and thus capable of unity with the whole communion of saints." Ratzinger, *Eschatology: Death and Eternal Life*, trans. Michael Waldstein (Washington, DC: Catholic University of America Press, 1998), 230.

8. Jonathan L. Kvanvig, "Hell," in Walls, *The Oxford Handbook of Eschatology*, 421.

9. G. C. Berkouwer, *The Return of Christ*, trans. James van Oosterom (Grand Rapids: Eerdmans, 1972), 393.

God's glory," that all things will be gathered up under Christ (Eph. 1:10), that God will be all in all (1 Cor. 15:28), or that every knee will bow and tongue confess that Jesus Christ is Lord (Phil. 2:10-11)?[10] Among academic theologians at least, it would be fair to say that commitment to an eternally populated hell has increasingly fallen on hard times. Regarding the duration of punishment, there has even been a significant revision of claims by evangelicals such as John Stott who have argued for temporary punishment followed by the annihilation of the reprobate. Moreover, a number have argued that texts regarding the universality of the eschatologically saving presence of the loving purposes of God support a case for the *apokatastasis* or universal salvation.[11] The debates between those arguing for eternal reprobation and those arguing for universal salvation continue unabated, and the biblical exegesis can appear rather tortured to the observer. On the other hand, other theologians argue that eschatological matters cannot be speculated on, since "the end of things, like their origin and essence, is unknown to us."[12] "We do not live, nor can we see, beyond the end of history. It is in time alone, the time that God has given us, that we are born, and live, [and] make plans."[13] Barth, Balthasar, and others claim that it is incumbent on Christians to hope for the reconciliation of all things in God's gift of renewing communion. Yet this is only to be hoped for, since it cannot be expected or asserted; hell remains a real threat for the disobedient. Even if all things—things past, present, and yet to come—are taken up into the coming of God in Christ, that will be experienced as hellish and not as eternal delight by those hardened in disobedience. Within such a perspective, hell is conceived as the result of God's taking seriously the sinful refusal of persons to be reconciled.

But it is not this state of eternal perdition that a Christian hopes for, nor hopes for as the fate of others. If hope is grounded in the God who is and promises to be for God's creatures in Christ, then images such as the *parousia* testify that hope is not for whatever a Christian wants, or thinks she wants;

10. Pannenberg, "The Task of Christian Eschatology," 11.

11. See 1 Cor. 15:22; Col. 1:19-20; Phil. 2:9-11; 1 Tim. 2:4-6. Some accounts of *apokatastasis*, such as those of John Hick or Nels Ferré, attempt to rescue the damning God from the charge of unjust cruelty in eternally torturing the wicked in a purely punitive action. Nonetheless, in these accounts God is portrayed in even more morally troubling terms, as one who uses all kinds of means (torture, shock therapy) in order to rehabilitate the wicked.

12. Herman Bavinck, *The Last Things: Hope for This World and the Next*, trans. John Vriend (Grand Rapids: Baker, 1996), 21.

13. Nicholas Lash, "Beyond the End of History," *Concilium* 5 (1994): 49.

nor is it hope for *things* such as peace, joy, life, and so on, at least not if they are abstracted from expectation for the cosmic fulfillment of the hospitably saving presence of God in Christ. Even so, while "we cannot bring in God's reign by our own efforts, . . . we can and should be encouraged by our hope in God to work for a world of greater justice, freedom, and peace," acting as witnesses to the coming consummation of God's rule in Christ.[14]

14. Migliore, *Faith Seeking Understanding*, 359.

Annotated Bibliography

I. General Resources

La Due, William J. *The Trinity Guide to Eschatology*. New York: Continuum, 2004.

La Due's short book is one of many accessible introductions to eschatological matters. It provides a survey divided into chapters on the biblical and historical background, classic Protestant approaches to eschatology in the twentieth century (Bultmann, Cullmann, Tillich), traditional Catholic approaches in the twentieth century (Rahner, Boros, Ratzinger), other related twentieth-century approaches (Küng, Hellwig, Balthasar), contemporary Protestant approaches (Robinson, Pannenberg, Moltmann), divergent voices (Macquarrie, Suchoki, and Hick), and three further approaches (Orthodox, liberationist, and feminist theologies). All short surveys have to be selective. In this volume, the discussion is substantially weighted toward twentieth-century theologians, although Karl Barth does not feature apart from an occasional mention, and the author pays little attention to the appearance of various forms of apocalyptic imagination through the twentieth century.

Mühling, Marcus. *T&T Handbook of Christian Eschatology*, trans. Jennifer Adams-Maßmann and David Andrew Gilland. London: T&T Clark, 2015.

Mühling identifies the shifts in modern eschatological discourse, from the seeming absence of engagement with eschatology at the outset of the twentieth century to the emergence of dogmatics wholly determined by eschatological themes mid-century. Mühling introduces eschatology as a way into theology as a whole, which privileges hope as a way of thinking and performing theology. Eschatology, then, is a form of reflective action in the present. His text is particularly instructive for its rendering of themes not usually considered native to modern systematic discussions of eschatology, such as liturgy and ethics. The first section of the book introduces a number of historical approaches to eschatology. The second section develops a set of suppositions grounding Christian eschatology in the doctrine of God and Christology. The third part examines what has been a perennial issue in modern eschatological accounts, the relation of time and eternity. Parts four and five deal explicitly with the systematic questions of millennialisms, death, judgment, the scope of salvation, the future of nonhuman creation, etc. These parts are woven together by Mühling's overriding concern that theology is to be conceived as action, and these doctrines are all to inform Christian performance.

Schwarz, Hans. *Eschatology.* Grand Rapids: Eerdmans, 2000.

Schwarz's informed and informative introduction to eschatology, focusing on the theme of eschatology and hope, is one of the best of the eschatology books published around the turn of the millennium. It covers the history of its topics from the biblical materials through to contemporary reflections, and it addresses death, immortality, resurrection, millenarianism, universal salvation, purgatory, heaven and hell, and the ethical demands of anticipating the coming of God's new world. Schwarz engages a wide range of thinkers on these themes. He also discusses a series of perceived pressures on Christian eschatology, from scientific developments (such as Darwinian evolution) to secular humanisms and nihilisms. Schwarz declares that, given the temptations in our world toward passive resignation and despair or wishful utopianism, "Christian eschatology is needed today, perhaps even more than ever, to provide for us both the perspective of the future and, even more importantly, a guiding light showing us how to pursue life meaningfully in the present" (p. xiii).

Walls, Jerry L., ed. *The Oxford Handbook of Eschatology.* Oxford: Oxford University Press, 2008.

This substantial volume is composed of thirty-nine chapters by a range of scholars who cover a vast array of eschatological themes and topics. The first part, "Historical Theology," covers biblical and patristic developments and perspectives. Noteworthy here are John J. Collins's and Christopher Rowland's contributions on "Apocalyptic Eschatology in the Ancient World" and "The Eschatology of the New Testament Church," respectively. Walls in his introduction and Brian Daley in his "Eschatology in the Early Church Fathers" address questions related to the understanding of eschatology as concerning the ending of things, or the last things. Five chapters cover "Eschatology in World Religions." The second part of the volume, "Eschatology in Distinct Christian Traditions and Theological Movements," includes chapters on Roman Catholic, Orthodox, Protestant, fundamentalist, Pentecostal and Charismatic, process, liberation, and feminist perspectives. The final part of the collection is entitled "Issues in Eschatology," and it includes chapters on such theological issues as millennialism, resurrection, and so on, in addition to an interesting assortment of philosophical and cultural issues. As with all collections, the quality of the contributions is variable, but it remains a useful introductory guide.

II. Biblical Resources

Borg, Marcus J. "An Orthodoxy Reconsidered: The 'End-of-the-World Jesus.'" In *The Glory of Christ in the New Testament: Studies in Christology in Memory of George Bradford Caird*, ed. L. D. Hurst and N. T. Wright, 207–17. Oxford: Clarendon, 1987.

Following G. B. Caird, Borg argues that Jesus did not proclaim the imminent end of the world. The main controversies Jesus was engaged in concerned his own people, and so he criticized the separatist group's purity code, carved out a path for peace in relation to the Roman occupation, practiced compassionate non-exclusion of the otherwise marginalized, and warned of the destructive consequences of the path his people were taking. Furthermore, Borg claims that the textual basis for the apocalyptic "Son of Man" sayings attributed to Jesus is overwhelmingly weak, and therefore they should no longer be seen as part of the authentic message of Jesus. Rather, they should be regarded as having been generated by the post-Easter Christian communities reflecting on Daniel 7:14. Borg asserts that Jesus, like his Jewish contemporaries, believed in the resurrection of the dead and the last judgment, but he was not proclaiming that this judgment was near. Borg claims that "the Easter event that triggered the belief that the end of the world was at hand," especially "coupled with the outpouring of the Spirit" (p. 214).

Borg, Marcus J. *Jesus in Contemporary Scholarship*. Valley Forge, PA: Trinity Press International, 1994.

This book develops more fully the thesis offered in Borg's earlier paper. Biblical scholars have long understood the original message of Jesus to be full of urgency and crisis, but contemporary scholarship has largely moved away from seeing Jesus as an eschatological prophet who proclaimed the imminent end of the world. Many scholars now maintain that the "coming of the Son of Man" sayings were not authentic to Jesus's preaching but were manufactured by the early Christian communities after Easter as texts referring to the second coming of Jesus as judge and vindicator of the church. Further, Borg claims, many have argued that Jesus's eschatology did not have a chronological, temporal reference to an end of time. "It is not clear that the coming of the kingdom in power [in Mark 9:1] refers to the end of the world; the verse permits a number of interpretations and is sometimes viewed as inauthentic" (p. 54). Accordingly, there is little sense of any disappointment of hopes for an imminent coming of the kingdom. Borg understands Jesus's language of the kingdom of God as a symbol referring to the royal rule, power, compassion, and justice of God. What is cardinal in Jesus's message, he says, is the presence of the sovereign power of God, and he urges his audience to respond by allowing their lives to be shaped by its presence.

Cullmann, Oscar. *Christ and Time: The Primitive Christian Conception of Time and History,* trans. F. V. Filson. Revised edition. London: SCM, 1962.

Swiss Lutheran biblical scholar Oscar Cullmann observes that, for Jesus and for the early Christians, the expectation of the imminent *parousia* is not the starting point of faith but a consequence of faith derived from what has already occurred. In his account of the biblical understanding of history, which conceives of eschatology as a linear and chronological concept, Cullmann finds a threefold linear schematization of time: before creation, from creation to *parousia,* and after the *parousia.* This threefold division is overlaid by a twofold "salvation history" division: the present age and the coming age. The decisive midpoint of the two-part time line is the coming of the Messiah, the messianic time of salvation and its miracles. Thus Jesus is decisively the center of time, and because of this we are now living in the final phase or the end-time before the *parousia.* That *parousia* will be a public and cosmic event and will, like the first decisive event, take place on earth. Certainly the early hope for an imminent *parousia* proved to be mistaken, but since the basis of expectation is the Christ who has already come, it makes no difference in principle whether the interval is short or long.

Cullmann, Oscar. *Immortality of the Soul or Resurrection of the Dead? The Witness of the New Testament.* London: Epworth, 1958.

The book is based on a series of lectures that Cullmann delivered at Harvard in 1954–1955, developing two of the themes of his earlier eschatological work. First, he argues that while Greek philosophers understood the soul to be immortal, the early Christians regarded it as not naturally immortal, but only becoming so through faith in the resurrection of Jesus Christ. Cullmann's second theme is that of the resurrection of the body. In contrast to the Hellenistic disjunction between soul and body, in which the soul is freed from the body when the body is destroyed, the New Testament teaches that persons who die in Christ are raised, transformed in the Holy Spirit on the last day by God's renewing act of new creation.

Dodd, C. H. *Parables of the Kingdom.* Revised edition. Glasgow: Collins, 1961.

This landmark work by Charles Harold Dodd (1884–1973), formerly the Norris

Hulse Professor of Divinity at the University of Cambridge, is in many ways a response to the so-called consistent eschatology of Johannes Weiss and Albert Schweitzer. Noting that "The parables are perhaps the most characteristic element in the teaching of Jesus as recorded in the Gospels" (p. 13), Dodd explores the significance of their message for understanding the nature of the momentous apocalyptic crisis manifested in and by Jesus's ministry. The tension is between the fact that Jesus announces that "'the Kingdom of God' is a present fact" and yet that the kingly rule of God "is something yet to be believed . . . [since the] world does not recognize Him as King" (p. 30). This is in accordance with the Jewish use of the kingly metaphor at the time. What distinguishes Jesus's preaching from that of others, however, is the way this kingdom is associated with Jesus himself, and this is forcefully articulated in his connection with the Danielic "Son of Man." Accordingly, the apocalyptic speculations miss the connection of Jesus's "realized eschatology" (p. 41) with the "hour of decision" (p. 148). The predictive element of Jesus's proclamations symbolically relates to the crisis that Jesus's message and his impending execution bring for the disciples, as well as the crisis that is looming for Israel under the Romans. Dodd understands Jesus's ethical teaching "not as 'interim ethics', but as a moral ideal for men who have 'accepted the Kingdom of God', and live their lives in the presence of His judgment and His grace, now decisively revealed" (p. 82). None of this involves dehistoricizing the encounter, however. Even though the Gospels offer no support for maintaining that the millennial kingdom will come after a long cycle of history, the enjoyment of divine blessedness "is never exhausted in any experience that falls within the bounds of time and space" (p. 156).

González, Catherine Gunsalus, and Justo L. González. *Revelation*. Louisville: Westminster John Knox, 1997.

The Gonzálezes' commentary focuses upon maintaining Revelation's significance for liberation in the present. This happens both when the text is seen as purely indicative of future events and equally when it becomes a historical relic. At the outset of the commentary the authors write that they are attempting to recover something of the dynamic poetic flow of the text, which was originally intended to be read aloud. "In order for readers of Revelation to understand this book even more fully, we must seek to discover and understand the references to the Hebrew scriptures and to the particular circumstances of that time. This is a painstaking work, which in itself interrupts the reading of the book as it was intended to be read. . . . For that reason, we must also read the book in a different fashion entire sections at a time, not worrying if there is a phrase or an image we do not understand, so as to recover something of the flow, rhythm and emotion with which it must have been first written and read" (p. 2). This poetic reading of the text is intended as a vehicle for displacing the privilege recently given to historical readings of the text.

Kovacs, Judith, and Christopher Rowland. *Revelation.* Oxford: Wiley Black-well, 2004.

Kovacs and Rowland's commentary is distinctive in its focus upon the interpretative significance of Revelation for the present. "In a time when the most prominent interpretations of the book emphasise its meaning for the past (historical criticism) or the future (prognostications of the *eschaton*), we aim to round out the picture by calling attention to interpreters who seek to articulate the book's meaning for the present" (p. 11). They draw particular attention to the way the Enlightenment has shaped readings of the text that are both purely historical and purely futurist, a result of the reluctance of Enlightenment exegetes to engage the more poetic and symbolic meanings of the text in an effort to maintain historical rigor. This commentary is intended to resist that tradition.

Mangina, Joseph L. *Revelation.* Grand Rapids: Brazos, 2010.

As a part of a series on the theological interpretation of Scripture, Mangina's commentary is committed to the idea that "dogma clarifies rather than obscures" (p. 11). This idea forms something of a counter-punch to modern exegetes who insist on maintaining a clear distinction between theological and historical work on the Scriptures. For many moderns following German historical criticism, to assume the truthfulness of credal truth claims *prior to* the beginning of the interpretative task was a fundamental hermeneutical *faux pas*. This is not to say, however, that Mangina does not undertake historical work. Throughout the text he draws upon the work of historical scholars, and he is careful to locate the original text in its original context. However, what makes this commentary distinctive among others on Revelation is the question of the context in which the text is read now, which is, for Mangina, the church. The text of Revelation is read as a liturgical and theologically instructive text. Mangina avoids futurist speculation and instead engages in a mode of interpretation that we have called "actualizing." Hence, he engages in extensive dialogue with contemporary politics, literature, and culture.

III. Patristic Resources

Daniélou, Jean. *Origen*, trans. Walter Mitchell. Eugene: Wipf and Stock, 1955.

Daniélou's reading of Origen's eschatology embeds it within the way Origen thinks about creation. "Eschatology corresponds to archaeology" (p. 176). All things have both their origin and their end in God, and yet the end of things is never accomplished in any straightforward manner, because the beginning is the infinite depth of the Father. Origen is the first in a long line of Greek-speaking fathers of the church who make much of this way of speaking about eschatology as a mystery that corresponds to the mysteriousness of God's own being. Daniélou suggests that there is little in the Scriptures to give substantive content to a concrete eschatological vision; consequently, we are "faced . . . with Origen's personal system in its most characteristic form" (p. 176). Hence, the fundamental metaphysical assumptions of Origen's system are on display in his eschatology. As all things proceed from God in God, so all things return to God in God. The world is imagined as a great classroom, and God as the master pedagogue, teaching his free creatures to inhabit the good.

Pseudo-Dionysius. *Pseudo-Dionysius: The Complete Works*, trans. Colm Luibheid and Paul Rorem. New York: Paulist, 1987.

In the late fifth and early sixth centuries a Byzantine philosopher-theologian wrote under the name of Dionysius the Areopagite, an Athenian converted to Christianity through the ministry of Paul (Acts 17:34). He was likely Syrian and a monk. Only four treatises and a series of letter are extant from these pseudonymous works, although the extant works refer to various others. His body of literature was translated into Latin in the ninth century, and as a result he gained a great reputation as an authority. Pseudo-Dionysius, also referred to as Pseudo-Denys, speaks of two ways of doing theology: a cataphatic approach (offering affirmations about God) and an apophatic approach (denying that God can be spoken of). These are not two successive stages, so that one can be left behind once the other has been achieved, but supplemental approaches. In fact, the apophatic is less a strategy or technique, even a branch of theology, than a mood or ethos. It removes all strategies, techniques, and systems in theology through articulating the inability of language and thought to depict and conceive of God. So Pseudo-Dionysius emphasizes the indescribability of God's nature, and he expresses this through self-negating claims, saying that God is "Superessential Essence" and "supra-existent Being" (*The Divine Names* 1.1, 588B). He uses the Neoplatonic prefix "supra" or "hyper," meaning "being beyond." God is not one being among others, not existent in the way they are existent as creatures. Rather, in God's nature, the inaccessible God is utterly different in kind, dwelling on a plane where there is nothing whatever beside God's self. God is thus "beyond being . . . above and beyond speech, mind, or being itself," "the Superunknowable" (*The Divine Names* 1.1, 588A, 593B). Consequently, Pseudo-Dionysius emphasizes the practice of Christian "unknowing," "the unknowing of what is beyond being" (*hyperousios*). But how does God come to be spoken of and not spoken of? By revelation, since God "alone could give an authoritative account of what [God] really is" (*The Divine Names* 1.1, 588B). This means that Pseudo-Dionysius's God is hidden, not because God is distant, but rather precisely in God's presence. And that presence is described as an ecstatic state of yearning love of creatures. Pseudo-Dionysius's favorite term for the Christian life is "anagogy" or "being led upward." This movement of transformative illumination involves the purificatory preparation for, and participation in, the creature's response to divine love in praise and worship. Pseudo-Dionysius refers to this as an "ascent" to God in "contemplation," "self-dispossession," or "undivided and absolute abandonment of yourself and everything" (a dying to self, as in Mark 8:34–35) (*The Mystical Theology* 1000A), and "union" and "communion" with God in which the believer is deified by grace. "The Good returns all things to itself and gathers together whatever may be scattered, for it is the divine Source and unifier of the sum total of all things. . . . All things are returned to it as their own goal" (*The Divine Names* 4.4, 700B).

Scott, Mark M. *Journey Back to God: Origen and the Problem of Evil.* Oxford: Oxford University Press, 2012.

Scott positions himself between older readings of Origen as indebted to Platonic philosophy to the detriment of any theological content, and more recent readings of Origen that downplay the significance of Platonism for his thought in order to locate Origen's use of philosophical and theological grammars of the problem of evil in a pedagogically driven movement of created beings back to God.

Tertullian. *The Shows (De spectaculis)*, trans. Rev. S. Thelwall, in *Ante-Nicene Fathers*, vol. 3, ed. Philip Schaff, https://www.ccel.org/ccel/schaff/anf03 .iv.v.i.html.

The eschatological assumptions of early Christians emerged in the shadow of the Roman Empire and the figurehead of its power, the emperor, or Augustus. Roman rule had come with the promise of peace, the *pax Romana*, in which the power of the empire served as a shield against those who would disrupt the Roman way of life. One way in which Roman rule was reinforced was through the performance of public spectacles of various kinds, representing to the people the power of Roman rule and the favor of the gods. These spectacles included gladiator fights, naval battles, fights between people and wild beasts, etc. As such, they served both as entertainment and as reinforcements of the power of an imperial way of life, typified in the stratification of social reality. In the second century, the Carthaginian lawyer and theologian Tertullian, having become a Christian, grew to despise these spectacles of violence. In this text he engages at times in a vitriolic rebuttal of the spectacles, condemning those who participate in them to the spectacle of divine eschatological judgment. The piece culminates with him picturing the end of all things as an inverted Roman spectacle: "But what a spectacle is that fast-approaching advent of our Lord, now owned by all, now highly exalted, now a triumphant One! . . . How vast a spectacle then bursts upon the eye! What there excites my admiration? what my derision? Which sight gives me joy? which rouses me to exultation?—as I see so many illustrious monarchs, whose reception into the heavens was publicly announced, groaning now in the lowest darkness with great Jove himself, and those, too, who bore witness of their exultation; governors of provinces, too, who persecuted the Christian name, in fires more fierce than those with which in the days of their pride they raged against the followers of Christ" (ch. 30).

IV. Medieval Resources

Boethius, Anicius Manlius Severinus. *The Consolation of Philosophy*, trans. W. V. Cooper. http://www.exclassics.com/consol/consol.pdf (accessed December 12, 2016).

This early five-book Christian Platonic text, one of the most influential Latin works of the Middle Ages, is a good example of the shifts in attitude toward eschatological matters in the late patristic and early medieval periods. Composed in a prison cell while Boethius awaited trial for composing an anti-Arian tractate, *On the Trinity*, the work takes the form of a conversation with Philosophy, personified as a woman, on the purposefulness of life, the nature of the good life, and true happiness. Several things are important to notice in this text. First, Boethius takes on the role of the seer, one who has been given insight into the nature of things and the meaning of circumstances of unjust suffering. Second, discussions of the purpose of life do not lead to consideration of millenarian or apocalyptic forms of hope; rather, they have to do with the way providence brings all things to a good outcome. Third, life is directed by providence toward the soul's seeking its Creator, the unchanging and ever-present eternal one, and away from evil, which is self-destructive. The quest of the good life is the pursuit of union with the very one who is the source of all goods and proper happiness. Lady Philosophy concludes: "God is ever the constant foreknowing overseer, and the ever-present eternity of His sight moves in harmony with the future nature of our actions, as it dispenses rewards to the good, and punishments to the bad. Hopes are not vainly put in God, nor prayers in vain offered: if these are right, they cannot but be answered. Turn therefore from vice: ensue virtue: raise your soul to upright hopes: send up on high your prayers from this earth. If you would be honest, great is the necessity enjoined upon your goodness, since all you do is done before the eyes of an all-seeing Judge" (70–71).

McGinn, Bernard. *Apocalypticism in the Western Tradition*. Collected Studies, 430. Aldershot: Variorum, 1994.

This collection of essays is focused chiefly on giving some contour to the notion of apocalyptic, a category hotly contested in recent scholarship. McGinn investigates figures and themes such as Bernard of Clairvaux, Joachim of Fiore, and the influence of papal power on the apocalyptic imagination. McGinn is particularly helpful in the way he distinguishes between general eschatology and apocalyptic. As he puts it, apocalyptic "announces details of the future course of history and the imminence of its divinely appointed end in a manner that manifestly goes beyond the mere attempt to interpret the Scriptures. New and more precise descriptions of the events are incorporated, frequently from a new revelatory source (the Sibyl was a popular one); and traditional eschatological imagery is made more vital by being applied directly to current historical events" (p. 254).

McGinn, Bernard, John J. Collins, and Stephen J. Stein, eds. *Encyclopedia of Apocalypticism.* Volume 2: *Apocalypticism in Western History and Culture.* London: Bloomsbury Academic, 2000.

This volume provides an introduction to various historical epochs, figures, and tropes in the history of apocalyptic literature. The material on the Middle Ages in particular is instructive as it locates the slow development of movements for imperial and ecclesial reform alongside the renewed vigor given to apocalyptic literature. This is particularly important as a way of locating the development of Reformation and modern forms of historical consciousness.

Meister Eckhart. *Meister Eckhart: Teacher and Preacher,* ed. and trans. Bernard McGinn. New York: Paulist, 1986.

Meister Eckhart forms the beginning of a tradition of German mysticism and philosophy that has continued to the present, including such figures as Luther, Hegel, Kierkegaard, and Heidegger. Of particular eschatological significance is the function of the language of *grund* (ground) in Eckhart's thought. Eckhart understands God to be the ground of all existence, and so both the beginning and the end of creaturely being. For Eckhart, a finite thing's finite hunger, or end, can be temporarily satisfied. However, it is "the opposite in things whose goal is infinite, for such things always hunger and thirst, and hunger more ardently and avidly the more they eat." Thus the creature participating in the infinite ground of being always hungers for more. "This is why it always thirsts for its superior's presence, and it is better and more proper to say that it continually receives its existence than that it has existence in itself in a fixed or even initial way" (p. 175). The creature is, then, always on a journey back to God that never concludes. This is similar to an idea in the Greek fathers whereby the creature is in "perpetual progress." This idea is grounded in the assumption that God is the one into whom the creature grows. Because God is infinite, the creature always has more growing to do. Eckhart is positioned in a very interesting way between the fathers and the moderns. Of particular significance with regard to eschatology is the way he is uninterested in historical speculations but recovers an interest in the formation of human persons in the good—God.

"The Spiritual Franciscans." In *Apocalyptic Spirituality: Treatises and Letters of Lactantius, Adso of Montier-en-Der, Joachim of Fiore, the Franciscan Spirituals, Savonarola*, ed. and trans. Bernard McGinn. New York: Paulist, 1979.

This is a collection of apocalyptic writings from the late Middle Ages, assembled, edited, and introduced by Bernard McGinn. The Franciscan Spirituals were a group concerned to radically embrace the vow of poverty fundamental to the Franciscan order. As McGinn notes, they understood "the meaning of his [St. Francis's] special devotion to poverty, and the historical significance of the order he founded, in terms of a theology based largely on the thought of Joachim of Fiore. The Calabrian abbot had not only predicted a key role for coming orders of his *viri spirituales* ('spiritual men') in the imminent crisis of history, but had also looked forward to a Millennial state of the Church on earth under the aegis of the most perfect form of the religious life" (p. 150). This meant that the Franciscan Spirituals became deeply invested in the imminent unfolding of history, and they used apocalyptic tropes to speak of the coming judgment and millennial age. This was amplified by the crisis of the Avignon papacy (1309-1377). For example, Peter John Olivi argues, "When we look at the order of the universe, the sacred law that Christ solemnly promulgated presents itself in many and admirable ways—'Unless the grain of wheat falls dead upon the ground, it will remain alone; if it has died, it will bear much fruit.' This law is the foundation of the whole process of natural change and movement according to which the corruption of one thing is the generation of another" (p. 173). The Joachimite overtones are apparent in Peter's insistence that the old time must come to an end and meet judgment before the new can begin. Already this hints at historicist themes that will become explicit in figures such as Karl Marx and G. W. F. Hegel. In wedding the natural, the theological, and the historical together, an apocalyptic vision of the future is born. This collection is particularly valuable in the way it shows how Joachimite thought works itself out in the lives of these religious as they confront what they consider to be corrupt ecclesial practice.

V. Reformations Resources

Bayer, Oswald. *Martin Luther's Theology: A Contemporary Interpretation*, trans. Thomas H. Trapp. Grand Rapids: Eerdmans, 2008.

Bayer's authoritative account of Luther is illustrative of the turn in more recent literature to the eschatological impulse in Luther's thought as a whole. Bayer identifies at the heart of Luther's thought a rupture between the old and the new aeon, which plays itself out in a number of ways. Bayer's Luther is concerned to confront what is most existentially urgent in the human situation, the reality of evil and the judgment of God. Luther's thought bears an intense apocalyptic thrust, as can be seen in the centrality of the theology of the cross to Luther's thought. That is, Luther's thought is concerned with the breaking in of the new in the cross of Christ, which ruptures all previous forms of power, domination, and control, revolutionizing the very ways in which we organize ourselves and speak about God. This then gives Bayer the ability to make sense of the relationship between hiddenness and revelation, world history and divine judgment, etc. God's action is not in continuity with the world, but is radically interrogative of our patterns of life and thought. This insight reverberates throughout the history of Protestantism in a number of different ways.

Luther, Martin. *On the Babylonian Captivity of the Church, 1520: The Annotated Luther Study Edition*, ed. Erik H. Hermann and Paul W. Robinson. Minneapolis: Fortress, 2016.

In this classic text, Martin Luther protests what he considers to be the abuses of the late medieval Roman Catholic Church in the selling of indulgences and the exclusion of the laity from the Eucharist. Luther deploys the eschatological and apocalyptic imagery of exile, captivity, the Antichrist, etc., in order to illustrate both the severity of the situation and its eschatological significance. As far as the former goes, Luther's identification of the pope with the Antichrist is highly evocative, for it creates a disjunction between visible ecclesial office and the reality of the gospel. The pope, the supposed head of the church, is dislocated from the church, and so the true church is under foreign rule, the rule of the devil. In the latter case, there is an implicit and explicit eschatological urgency to Luther's call. Luther believes that divine judgment is always near, and his apocalyptic imagery is illustrative of this. A battle is taking place that is not immediately apparent. He calls for the church to embrace again the way of the cross, which is to set aside the trappings of power and its abuse in favor of a life shaped by sacrifice for the sake of others. For the *real* battle is between those who embrace the way of the cross and those who embrace the pursuit of vainglory.

Müntzer, Thomas. *The Collected Works of Thomas Müntzer*, trans. and ed. Peter Matheson. Edinburgh: T&T Clark, 1988.

This volume illustrates with great clarity the importance of Thomas Müntzer in the development of various radical traditions in Protestant thought. Included here are Müntzer's letters to various figures, including Martin Luther, illustrating the distinctive variety developing within Protestantism, particularly as Protestant leaders respond in varying ways to the Peasants' War. Müntzer's apocalypticism and political radicalism are on display, particularly his insistence that the political situation was reflective of the very end of days. Pertinent in this regard is *The Prague Protest*, wherein Müntzer explicitly styles himself as the inheritor of Jan Hus's Reformation and as an apocalyptic prophet. Müntzer's revelations differentiate his Reformation from Luther's and Calvin's in a quite distinctive manner. Whereas Luther had called the ecclesial hierarchy to account for its abuse of the scriptural text, Müntzer appeals to personal revelations. These revelations are intended as proof of his status as a prophet of the end of days. This locates Müntzer at the root of forms of Protestant theology, such as pietism, that emphasize experience. As different radical reformations took root across Europe, and as the Puritans took flight to the United States of America, various forms of emotivism attached to the election of the individual. Müntzer's influence can be traced in a number of different directions: to Friedrich Schleiermacher, who insisted on the priority of the "feeling of absolute dependence" in dogmatic work; to Jonathan Edwards's work on the religious affections; and to various apocalyptic political movements that looked to a charismatic leader.

Strohl, Jane E. "Luther's Eschatology." In *The Oxford Handbook to Martin Luther*, ed. Robert Kolb et al., 353–62. Oxford: Oxford University Press, 2009.

This piece helpfully describes some of the basic insights of Martin Luther's eschatology framed in terms of the traditional dogmatic categories surrounding the last things. Strohl illustrates Luther's relatively uncontroversial views on resurrection, the afterlife, judgment, etc. Her discussion of the secondary literature remains light and does not grapple with the ways in which the tenor of Luther's entire corpus has been cast in more recent decades by a total eschatological orientation. Strohl's discussions of Luther's vision of history are also rather simplified and fail to make sense of his later speculations, as well as the ontological grammar in which his vision of history is cast. Overall, although the essay offers little by way of an interpretative contribution in its own right, this is a helpful piece in that it points the reader to Luther himself.

VI. Early Modern Resources

Brightman, Thomas. *The Revelation of St. John, Illustrated with Analysis and Scholions, Wherein the Sence Is Opened by the Scripture; And the Events of Things Foretold, Shewed by Histories; Together With a Most Comfortable Exposition of the Last and Most Difficult Part of the Prophecy of Daniel.* Amsterdam: Thomas Stafford, 1644.

The Church of England ruled in its Forty-Two Articles of Religion (1552) that millenarianism was unacceptable Anglican teaching. However, by the mid-seventeenth century millenarianism had gained considerable popularity, and it contributed to the English political revolution and the civil war. Country clergyman Thomas Brightman (1562–1607) published commentaries on Daniel, Revelation, and the Canticles intending to prove the imminence of a joyous new age, and importantly revisioning John Foxe's eschatology. In his apocalyptic interpretation of history, Brightman regarded the prophecies of Revelation 20 as having been fulfilled when Emperor Constantine created the conditions of imperial peace for the church. At the end of this millennial period the devil was unleashed, as evidenced in the Turkish advances. The first resurrection that occurred was a spiritual resurgence of faithfulness among reforming elements within the church, associated with John Wycliff, among others. Brightman dated this millennium around 1300. In his view, the pope is the Antichrist who will be divinely damned. However, in 1650 the power of the Turkish Empire and the Roman Catholic Church would begin to dissipate, and it would be followed by the national conversion of the Jewish people. The second resurrection would involve the return of the Jews to Palestine and their conversion. After 2300 the consummation will be established.

Edwards, Jonathan. *History of Redemption*. In *The Works of Jonathan Edwards*, vol. 9. New Haven: Yale University Press, 1989.

In this work deriving from sermons of 1738–1739 and his experience of the so-called Great Awakening, Edwards tells the story of salvation from its beginning to his own day. The biblical prophecies depict the sweep of history in seven periods, which Edwards understands in terms of the sequential pouring out of the seven bowls or vials of God's wrath against the beast of Revelation 16. As was common among Protestants of the period, Edwards portrays the papacy as the Antichrist, which will fall before the subjugation of the Muslims and the conversion of the Jews, the enlightening and conversion of the whole heathen world, and the inauguration of the last judgment and the prosperous state of the church. Unlike many of his contemporaries, Edwards did not believe that further catastrophic persecution of the church was necessary—the Great Awakening was a foretaste and sign of the commencement of the church's millennial prosperity. (He was to temper that optimistic portrayal later in his life.) Elsewhere in his writings he tellingly opposed those who predicted future catastrophe on the grounds that the pessimism of this expectation would undermine prayer and evangelism. Nor did he believe that an exact timetable for understanding God's eschatological action could be made.

Gribben, Crawford. *The Puritan Millennium: Literature and Theology, 1550–1682*. Revised edition. Eugene: Wipf and Stock, 2008.

Gribben argues that Puritanism was an intensely eschatological movement. From the beginning, the Puritans developed eschatological interests in a wide diversity of contexts and for quite distinctive reasons, some of which were conflicting. They possessed a reformist agenda because of the kinds of eschato-logical hopes by which they were shaped. For example, the execution of King Charles I was motivated by a radical millenarian eschatology in order to clear the way for the coming of Christ, England's rightful king. The book offers a series of readings of texts by John Foxe, James Ussher, George Gillespie, John Rogers, John Milton, and John Bunyan.

Mede, Joseph. *The Key of the Revelation*, trans. Richard More. London: Mifflin, 1966.

In his day a celebrated biblical scholar and professor of Greek at Cambridge, the Englishman Joseph Mede (1586–1638) published his *Clavis Apocalyptica* in Latin in 1627 only for private circulation, but it ended up becoming influential and much admired. Translated into English in 1643 with the title *A Key to the Apocalypse*, the book drew detailed correspondences between historical events and the images in the book of the Apocalypse, to end with the Jewish destruc-tion of the papacy, the battle of Armageddon that prepares the earth for Christ's millennial reign, and the resurrection of the martyrs. Such expectations of a dawning new age fueled revolution in the colonies against "Old England" and won Mede followers, including John Milton, Henry More, and Isaac Newton, among many others in England, the European continent, and North America.

Napier, John. *A Plaine Discovery of the Whole Revelation of Saint John*. Edin-burgh: Walde-grave, 1593.

John Napier (1550–1617) was a Scottish mathematician. He wrote this influ-ential commentary on the Apocalypse in an attempt to demonstrate that the fulfillment of history was a regular, observable, and thus normal process. He believed that the thousand years of Satan's binding began around 300 CE, and this inaugurated the Antichrist's reign over Christians. The latter Napier iden-tified with the birth of the state church, and on the back of that he criticized the political and religious presuppositions of both the British government and its established churches. Within limits, future events of certain kinds could be predicted mathematically, and so he transformed the biblical reader from an exegete into a seer. Napier estimated that the seventh trumpet, signaling the end of God's dealings with the world, had begun to sound in 1541 and would end by 1786.

VI. Modern Resources

Balthasar, Hans Urs von. *The Glory of the Lord: A Theological Aesthetics*, vol. 1: *Seeing the Form*, trans. Erasmo Levia-Merikakis. San Francisco: Ignatius, 1982.

Hans Urs von Balthasar famously begins his magisterial theological trilogy with a theological aesthetic. The first volume is concerned to locate the christological "form" of this project, and it concludes with an eschatological reflection. For Balthasar, the world is, insofar as it is eschatologically given to participate in the Logos, "a sacred theophany" (p. 679). This does not take place in any kind of panentheism or pantheism, but by the logic of the hypostatic union, the union of God and humanity in the person of Jesus Christ. In this sense, then, the world is always on its way back to God. It is being lured, transformed, and remade by the working of God's Logos and Spirit to the end that, eschatologically, it will both participate fully in the divine communion and be wholly transfigured into the *image* of God. Accordingly, Balthasar's "eschatological reduction," by which he concludes the first volume of his aesthetic, sets up the rest of the volumes. As Balthasar continues he will narrate the gradual loss of analogical vision in the West, and thereby the loss of an eschatological horizon for human life. His aesthetic is the restoration of that vision, grounded in the Logos, by the working of the Spirit.

Balthasar, Hans Urs von. *Dare We Hope "That All Men Be Saved"? With a Short Discourse on Hell*, trans. David Kipp and Lothar Krauth. San Francisco: Ignatius, 2014.

One of Balthasar's more controversial texts, this piece is an exploration of the possibility of the *hope* that all humanity will be saved. Crucially, Balthasar is more interested in identifying the reasons for hope than in predicting an eschatological future. This is a fine line, but an important one. He is interested in the logic internal to the gospel that would allow one to be cautiously optimistic that God may well be even more generous than we had perhaps dared to imagine. In order to do this he examines classic figures such as Origen, Augustine, and Thomas; the biblical materials; and the theological logics of evil, death, and hell. Balthasar's logic is in many ways consistent with much of his other work, and it resembles some of Karl Barth's reservations over an unabashed universalism. While Balthasar argues that there is the possibility of hope, that hope is as yet unrealized and can never become a necessity. We cannot lock divine action into a form of logical necessity and fail to appreciate the intractable problems of human and divine freedom.

Barth, Karl. *Epistle to the Romans*, trans. E. C. Hoskyns. Oxford: Oxford University Press, 1933.

The second edition of Karl Barth's *Epistle to the Romans* is one of the decisive texts of twentieth-century theology. Dropping "like a bomb on the playground of the theologians," as Karl Adam once said, this piece decisively indicated Barth's break from the nationalism of many of his teachers. Aghast as many of his most admired teachers signed the infamous 1914 *Manifesto of the 93*, a letter of support for Kaiser Wilhelm II's declaration of war, Barth turned to the apostle Paul, Kierkegaard, Dostoevsky, Nietzsche, Overbeck, and others for assistance. The result was a first edition of the commentary published in 1919 and a significantly revised version in 1922. The second edition is particularly decisive for the development of twentieth-century apocalyptic. Barth often uses sharp dialectical imagery in order to illustrate, in rather Lutheran fashion, the utter discontinuity of the divine Word with the word of his culture. He employs various military images, both in order to echo the war and so as to bring to bear the severity of divine judgment. Soaked in the apocalyptic feeling surrounding World War I, this text oozes with the urgency of the church's task. As the great empires of Europe finally come to destroy one another, and as the world collapses in on itself, Barth turns to an alternate order initiated in the catastrophic good news of the cross.

Bauckham, Richard, and Trevor Hart. *Hope against Hope: Christian Eschatology in Contemporary Context.* London: Darton, Longman & Todd, 1999.

This book is shaped in many ways as an apologetic exercise. Bauckham and Hart describe a wide range of secular hopes and analyze the pressures that have been put on them. They explore Christian theological resources in order to offer a sustainable alternative, a "hope against hope." This is a hope shaped by the crucified and raised Jesus, the site of the newness of God's faithful healing of creation. The contrast, then, is between "transcendent possibilities of God the Creator who gives his creation future" and "hope in the merely immanent possibilities of human history that now threaten the future as much as they promise to create it" (p. xi). New life comes in and through God's action of promised renewal of all things. The ideology of progress in particular is subjected to critique. These hopes for life have turned dark and deadly as a result of the horrors of the twentieth century. To this useful analysis one must add that, despite the dark turn, some forms of progressivism continue to capture the imaginations of many in the contemporary world.

Blaising, Craig A., and Darrel B. Bock. *Progressive Dispensationalism.* Grand Rapids: Baker, 1993.

While John Darby and Charles Scofield's dispensationalism attained enormous popular success, it has come under increasing pressure in academic circles. *Progressive Dispensationalism* is an attempt to think carefully about the relationship between language of "dispensation" and "covenant" in the scriptural texts in order to rethink the categories of traditional and classical dispensa-tionalism. Whereas traditional dispensationalism describes a series of separate dispensations in history, each one bracketed by a period of judgment, pro-gressive dispensationalism sees continuity between dispensations. Bock and Blaising speak of a single covenant with a series of partial fulfillments. They also maintain a premillennial, pretribulation eschatology and insist upon the historical-grammatical method of interpretation. This remains in continuity with earlier forms of dispensationalism. Progressive dispensationalism should not be confused with any form of political progressivism. "Progressive" in this instance is functioning purely as a description of how dispensations progress and overlap with one another.

Dussel, Enrique. *Philosophy of Liberation*, trans. Aquilina Martinez and Chris-tine Morkosky. Maryknoll: Orbis, 1980.

Dussel's *Philosophy of Liberation*, along with other texts such as Paulo Freire's *Pedagogy of the Oppressed*, is an example of the broad impact that notions of liberation have had on Latin American thought throughout the last century. Dussel's work is essential to understanding much of the philosophical infra-structure of liberation theology. Gutiérrez and others have been interested in notions of "place" in eschatology, rather than simply the temporal dimensions of eschatological language. Dussel's philosophy informs this. He states, "Euro-pean philosophy has given almost exclusive preponderance to temporality. No wonder it has now given privileged place to the fundamentality of the future in its emphasis on *Entwurf* [outline] and the *Prinziphoffnung* [principle of hope]. This philosophy must be understood well, and its snares must be discovered. . . . To give prominence to future temporality is to give privileged place to what we are already" (p. 24). Dussel's point is that Western hegemony is blind to the fact that it is built upon the oppression of the poor. Because this is the case, the idea of the amplification of current conditions is not cause for hope for the poor at all. Yet it is precisely this kind of amplification of current conditions that the idea of a historically realized hope runs the risk of suggesting. Dussel, then, along with others, proposes that we find other ways to speak of the conditions for the possibility of hope. To think about hope as spatial as well as temporal is to think of how the social order might be radically changed here and now. It is to disavow oppression.

Eagleton, Terry. *Hope without Optimism*. Charlottesville: University of Virginia Press, 2015.

One common and important task is to understand what hope is in relation to optimism. In a discussion that covers a vast range of literature, philosophy, the-ology, and politics, Eagleton asserts that optimism attempts to buy hope on the cheap. Somewhat echoing Dietrich Bonhoeffer's distinction between costly and cheap grace in *The Cost of Discipleship*, Eagleton announces that hope is costly. Optimism is a "belief" (p. 1). This way of putting the matter may be a little misleading, however. After all, hope is bound up with a variety of beliefs—beliefs about the world, about the hopers' place in it, and about the range of possibilities that can be hoped for. Eagleton has something different in mind. In his view, optimism is characterized by a premature claim to knowing what is to come, a belief that things work out for the best, or that all shall be well, that flies in the face of the evidence. Optimism, then, refuses to countenance resistant facts. Moreover, it is based on the way the optimist *feels* and is thus "purely arbitrary" (p. 3). As such it is not a virtue. It cannot be cultivated, and it is not sustained by rational reflection. Finally, optimism tends toward moral inertia: "optimists are conservatives because their faith in a benign future is rooted in their trust in the essential soundness of the present. Indeed, optimism is a typical component of ruling-class ideologies" (p. 4). This means that optimism is complicit with forces that spread around misery, including the suffering and deaths that occur in the name of progress. In contrast, "authentic hope . . . needs to be underpinned by reason" (p. 3). It is honest, and brutally so if it is not to carry with it the hidden presence of an optimistic disposition. Hope is dissatisfied with the way things are and therefore a crucial component of transformative action. "Hope is thus a species of permanent revolution, whose enemy is as much political complacency as metaphysical despair" (p. 69). It is somewhat fragile in that it operates without guarantees, and properly so, since "there is no guarantee that love and justice will flourish on this side of the Parousia" (p. 34). Finally, hope is a virtue since it is a disposition, rather than an experience or a feeling, and can be cultivated and practiced in honest self-discipline. In theological terms, hope moves to resurrection only through crucifixion.

Fiddes, Paul S. *The Promised End: Eschatology in Theology and Literature.* Oxford: Blackwell, 2000.

Through considerable engagement with a range of important pieces of literature, Fiddes critically assesses a number of eschatological motifs. Prominent here are the images of hope, death, *parousia*, resurrection, time and eternity, waiting, and the millennium. His concern is to prevent eschatology from foreclosing the future so that hope can be held open. The conversation between theology and literature allows for the development of a model for texts that are inexhaustibly "open to new meaning which is to come to them in the future, and also . . . 'seriously' open to the horizon which death gives to life" (p. 6). For Fiddes, following Frank Kermode, the universe has a story. The book advocates a theology of participation in the communion of God's own life, a sharing that the Spirit gives in "newness towards each other and to the future" (p. 204).

Gray, John. *Black Mass: Apocalyptic Religion and the Death of Utopia.* London: Penguin Books, 2007.

The book calls into question utopian beliefs in historical progress. The target is largely beliefs that have emerged since the Enlightenment, particularly the optimism of the Enlightenment itself, Communism, Nazism, and Neo-conservatism and Neoliberalism. All are secular forms of religious and mythological belief, and they are inevitably violent. Gray interprets Christianity as rather monolithic in its origins as a dualistic and violent apocalyptic movement, claiming that "early Christian myths of Apocalypse gave rise to a new kind of faith-based violence" (p. 4), an account largely developed from Albert Schweitzer's dated reading of the primitive Christian environment. Accordingly, Augustine's markedly different account is rather too cavalierly attributed not so much to his Christian heritage but to his Platonizing reformulation of Christianity. The book is, however, considerably more insightful when, working from Norman Cohn's reading of modernity, it interrogates the myth of human progress that continues to drive political policy and planning, especially in regard to the free market economy. Gray identifies and analyzes the eschatological mythology driving these policies and plans: "The political violence of the modern West can only be understood as an eschatological phenomenon" (p. 48). In this regard, Gray explains, the problem is that Christianity has given birth to "secular regimes that aimed to remake humanity by force" (p. 49), and this includes even the support of the free market economy (including its violent spread) by the likes of Margaret Thatcher. "Detached from religion and at the same time purged of the doubts that haunted its classical exponents, the belief in the market as a divine ordinance became a secular ideology of universal progress that in the late twentieth century was embraced by international institutions" (p. 105). However, "religion" has not disappeared entirely from the geopolitical setting, as can be seen in a chapter tracing the apocalyptic forms of utopianism that shaped the policy of the administration of George W. Bush with regard to the Middle East. Gray sees these policies as an attempt to impose American-style "universal democracy" and to build a worldwide economic system in its wake. The author also includes a helpful account of the apocalyptic beliefs of the English revolutionaries of the seventeenth century. The book does not articulate a coherently positive account of hope in any way that unites people in a common humanizing enterprise. Instead, it is prone to the kind of despair over the "common good" that is indebted to the political philosophy of Thomas Hobbes. So, while not uncritical of Hobbes's work, Gray argues in his final chapter that "Hobbes is a more reliable guide to the present than the liberal thinkers who followed" (p. 269).

Griffin, David Ray. "Process Eschatology." In *The Oxford Handbook to Eschatology,* ed. Jerry L. Walls. Oxford: Oxford University Press, 2010.

Griffin's essay outlines many of the major contours of Alfred North Whitehead's thought and develops some eschatological possibilities left open by Whitehead. The discussion of the possibility of an afterlife, given Whitehead's ambivalence, is particularly illuminating. Griffin argues that along with the Whiteheadian notion of God's "objective immortality" (see Whitehead's *Process and Reality* below), process thought also requires a doctrine of "subjective immortality" in order to be adequate to Christian concerns for a resurrection of the human person at the end of all things. He asserts that it is possible to think of the persistence of the human person beyond death because of the way Whitehead speaks of "panexperientialism," which defies any strict naturalist materialism. For Whitehead, all things experience, and yet there is a distinction between "genuine individuals, which have a unified experience, and the aggregational society of individuals (such as rocks, stars, and computers), which do not" (p. 304). This distinction allows Griffin to speak of the persistence of the mind as the aggregation of the whole experiencing human subject.

Gutiérrez, Gustavo M. "Notes for a Theology of Liberation." *Theological Studies* 31 (1970), 243–61.

Liberation theologies in Latin America grew out of the conviction that the underclass was being oppressed and exploited by the violent forces of capitalism and colonialism and the church's complicity in these forces. First and foremost, then, liberation theologies were concerned with *praxis*, that is, the concrete, practical forms of resistance to these forces under way in small "base communities." The language of *praxis*, adopted from Marxist sources, is an attempt to indicate the practical character of the aims of liberation theologies. Peruvian theologian Gustavo Gutiérrez argues that in liberation theologies we are dealing with the nature of the church's presence in the world, and the "principal fact about that presence today, especially in underdeveloped countries, is the participation by Christians in the struggle to create a just and fraternal society in which men can live in dignity and be masters of their own destiny" (p. 243). Rejecting the language of development, and its colonial overtones, he argues that "'liberation' seems more exact and richer in overtones" (p. 243). In this sense, then, for Gutiérrez, theology is a reflection upon the existential struggle for liberation and justice at work in communities of faith. Gutiérrez identifies three levels of activity for liberation theologians: first, the sociopolitical level, which is concerned with the conditions and structural problems facing communities in the present; second, the historical level, which looks to history as a space for the possibility of changed conditions; third, the transcendental level, which looks to the final reconciliation of all things with their creator, God. The eschatological functions on all three levels, as a change in "place," a historical change, and a change in relation to God. The first of these is perhaps the most interesting contribution Gutiérrez has made to contemporary theology, as he insists on disrupting the ways Western eschatologies have been preoccupied with history and time at the expense of space. This additional perspective, for Gutiérrez, suggests a way of escape from colonial narratives.

Harnack, Adolf von. *What Is Christianity?*, trans. Thomas Bailey Saunders. New York: Harper & Row, 1957.

Adolf von Harnack was the most accomplished church historian of his generation, famous particularly for his massive multi-volume series, *The History of Dogma*. The volume translated into English as *What Is Christianity?* was the product of a series of lectures on the essence of Christianity delivered at the University of Berlin during the winter term of 1899–1900. Following Albrecht Ritschl, Harnack attempted to develop a theological account that would be firmly grounded in the scientific discipline of history, and therefore what "is of permanent validity" (p. 14). This would be the "essence" of Christianity, the kernel detectable within the husk, the original message of Jesus freed from the stifling and superstitious conditions of church dogma. What is that essence? A little cryptically, he declares, "Eternal life in the midst of time, by the strength and under the eyes of God." Christianity, he explains, is not "a question of 'doctrine' being handed down by uniform repetition or arbitrarily distorted; it is a question of a *life*, again and again kindled afresh, and now burning with a flame of its own" (p. 11). Harnack summarizes Jesus's authentic and still relevant message as having been threefold: first, the kingdom of God and its coming; second, God the Father and the infinite value of the human soul; and third, the higher righteousness and the commandment of love. Harnack admits that Jesus's message of the kingdom embraces two poles: it is a purely future event and the external rule of God; and it is "something inward, something which is already present and making its entrance at the moment" (p. 52). However, these are not equitable. The former is a reflection of his Jewish heritage, whereas the latter is distinctively his. Accordingly, "the kingdom of God comes by coming to the individual, by entering into his soul and laying hold of it. True, the kingdom of God is the rule of God; but it is the rule of the holy God in the hearts of individuals; *it is God himself in his power*" (p. 56). In Harnack's account, the kingdom is individualized and interiorized. This, above all, is exemplified in Jesus's teaching in the Sermon on the Mount. Moreover, the kingdom is realized by human moral action for one's neighbor.

Hauerwas, Stanley. *Approaching the End: Eschatological Reflections on Church, Politics, and Life.* Grand Rapids: Eerdmans, 2013.

In this book the Christian ethicist Stanley Hauerwas attempts to appreciate "the significance of eschatology for understanding how Christians are to negotiate the world" (p. ix). His overriding concern is that churches fail to "be church," that "the business they are in may have only a very accidental relation with Christianity" (p. x). Such a problem manifests itself in a number of ways, such as in the succumbing of church life to the values of "choice" and thereby to the values of the market. Another is the way Christians have come to enjoy social and political status as a result of not taking "their Christian identity so seriously that they might destabilize the social order by, for example, challenging the presumption that war is a necessity if democracies are to survive" (pp. x–xi). For Hauerwas, these disorders are reflections of Christians having made peace with, and their home in, the world. Eschatology, however, provides a sense of living between the times and enables us to see the church's existence as "an alternative to the politics of the world" (p. xii). Among other things, this means that, "rightly understood, every loci of the Christian faith has an eschatological dimension, making impossible any isolated account of eschatology" (p. xii). In this way, the book discusses a number of issues from within an eschatological key so as to articulate Hauerwas's "deepest conviction that Christianity is training in how to be human" (p. xvii). On natural law, which he believes is justified by an account of the doctrine of creation that is insufficiently ethical, Hauerwas claims that "creation was . . . God's determinative act of peace" (p. 21); accordingly, it provides the conditions for a peaceable imagination so as to refuse the despair that underlies violence. On the political significance of apocalyptic, he declares that "the politics of apocalyptic simply *is* the existence of a people who refuse to acknowledge the claims of worldly rulers to be kings" (p. 26). One implication is that, by being faithful to the apocalyptic lordship of Jesus Christ, the church's witness must resist the tendency of rulers of states to treat other states simply as enemies to be fought and defeated. Moreover, this apocalyptic account refuses to understand the state as giving the church time, when, in contrast, it is God who gives the world time in order that the crucified and risen Jesus Christ may be preached to the end of the earth. According to Hauerwas, "to be a Christian requires training that lasts a lifetime" (p. 67). The book offers training in how to see things Christianly and thereby offers retraining away from the false sentimentalities and spiritualities that trivialize lives that are to be shaped by the crucified and risen Lord.

Healy, Nicholas J. *The Eschatology of Hans Urs von Balthasar: Being as Communion.* Oxford: Oxford University Press, 2005.

Healy's account of Hans Urs von Balthasar sets Balthasar's project within an eschatological frame from the outset of his career and illustrates the ways in which eschatological themes continually weave in and out of one another in Balthasar's thought. This book is particularly instructive in the way it illustrates how Balthasar's reading of the problems facing modernity play out eschatologically. So, in the sundering of theology from philosophy and of nature from grace in the late Middle Ages, resulting in the loss of an analogical world picture, modernity falls slowly into a form of immanentism. The "soul" of western culture is lost, and so the reference of all things to their ultimate end in God is lost. Balthasar's recovery of an analogical world picture is, then, for Healy, the slow recovery of the communion of all things with God, which is the ultimate "end" of all things.

Hick, John. *Death and Eternal Life.* London: Collins, 1976.

Hick explains the emergence of human life and consciousness as having two distinctive stages. The first, he explains in accordance with the best of nineteenth-century evolutionism, took many hundreds of millions of years of biological evolution to produce humanity in the divine image. This was only the raw material for the second stage of the creative process, which is the coming of free persons into the finite likeness of God, "the completed humanization of man in a society of mutual love" and awareness of the divine (p. 48). This evolutionary process nonetheless takes place against a backdrop of exertion, choice, struggle, conflict, and danger—a claim reminiscent of Tennyson's "Nature, red in tooth and claw"—with the process being depicted as a constant struggle against a hostile environment and savage violence against one's fellow human beings. With the exception of a few saints, human beings generally do not evolve fully in this life and thereby find their eschatological fulfillment in perfect likeness to the universal love of God. Yet the doctrine of hell is morally intolerable. Therefore, Hick speculates, this ultimate universal condition occurs over a number of future "lives," each separated by the clause-differentiating comma of death—fulfillment of the soul-making or person-making process of existence through the persuasive love of God.

Jüngel, Eberhard. *Death: The Riddle and the Mystery*, trans. Iain and Ute Nicol. Edinburgh: Saint Andrews, 1975.

Jüngel explores the way death rules over people's lives and therefore the impact it has as something greater than simply the mere act of passing away (though he does not address what kind of "act" it is). "It shapes man's life at its most fundamental level," he argues, "and determines him in the most human of his relationships" (p. 5). While nothing is certain or guaranteed in our lives, death at least is. That means that it has to be regarded as "an inalienable part of us" (p. 9). A crucial question, however, has to do with how Christian hope has to appropriately confront mortality, in either its natural or unnatural (unjustly imposed) forms. Grounding hope in the death (and to a somewhat lesser degree, resurrection) of Jesus Christ, Jüngel refuses to dislocate death and life from bodiliness or history. Therefore, "we should . . . be rightly suspicious of all those views of 'eternal life' which conceive of it as a kind of heavenly compensation for earthly renunciation and as in this sense involving the dissolution of the temporal limitations of human life" (p. 120). In contrast, Jüngel conceives of resurrected life as the saving of persons in the lives they have lived, and not the salvation of persons *out of* their finite, mortal, and relational lives. Accordingly, he argues, "Resurrection of the dead means then that it is the life we have actually lived that is gathered into community, made eternal and made manifest" (p. 121). Those raised in Christ are raised to new life in relationship to God, others, and themselves. Jüngel maintains "that there is definite work to be done to improve those conditions prevailing in the world which shape and regulate our lives" (pp. 132–33).

Keller, Catherine. *Apocalypse Now and Then: A Feminist Guide to the End of the World*. Minneapolis: Fortress, 2005.

Keller is interested in the development of primarily modern forms of apocalyptic and their political importance. As the subtitle suggests, feminist concerns are central to her work. She is concerned, therefore, that apocalyptic imagery often serves to fuel forms of patriarchal violence, visions of a violent God whose only weapon against violence in the world is counter-violence. Consequently, she develops a vision that is counter-apocalyptic rather than anti-apocalyptic, indicating her fear that simply saying no to apocalyptic is itself a form of apocalyptic in the way it breaks absolutely with it. This vision involves employing resources from process and feminist thought in order to affirm an emergent pneumatology, which is the affirmation of "finitude without end" (p. 274). Along the way, however, there are fascinating discussions of often neglected margins of apocalyptic thought, engagements with diverse philosophical figures such as Ernst Bloch and Friedrich Engels, and provocative engagements with the dynamics of contemporary politics and modern eschatological alarmism.

McDowell, John C. *The Gospel according to Star Wars: Faith, Hope and the Force*, chapter 8. Louisville: Westminster John Knox, 2007.

In George Lucas's epic cinematic saga, the wisdom of the Jedi imagines a way of living that necessarily supports considerations of flourishing together. Any hope generated on these grounds does protect hopers from despair, but only because it does not allow the hopers to focus on their own emotional state. The Jedi are called to a never-ending self-dispossessiveness that subverts their need for possessive guarantees, instead enabling them simply to live faithfully into their futures for the sake of the flourishing of all things. As Qui-Gon Jinn asserts in *The Phantom Menace*, "I will do what I must." This is a hope that is aware of a tragic quality of existence but that attempts to live the best possible life within the limits of one's existence. In this way, the *Star Wars* saga may be more theologically and ethically interesting than viewers who banally reduce it to entertainment pure and simple may imagine.

McDowell, John C. *The Politics of Big Fantasy: Studies in Cultural Suspicion.* Jefferson, NC: McFarland, 2014.

According to Frederic Jameson, American science fiction has a particular affinity with the dystopian rather than the utopian imagination, resulting from a cultural atrophy in which the future cannot be constructively imagined. Nonetheless, dystopian movies of a certain type can function as mediating lenses through which to critically interrogate beliefs, values, and decisions that are deemed to have catastrophic consequences for the nature of human identity. As such, dystopian movies play into cultural concerns about dehumanizing conditions in late modernity, as the self and society become problematically mediated in and through cultural regulations of the bureaucratizing, homogenizing, and commodifying of social life. The third chapter presses the sociopolitical critique of the dystopian imagination, but does so by assuming a variety of different types of dystopianism. While discussing a number of dystopian movies, this chapter specifically focuses on the Wachowski brothers' film *The Matrix*, arguing that it subverts its own critical dystopian potential and thereby slides back into celebrating the problematic realities it attempts to criticize. The movie's sequels push the series toward a flashy nihilism, only to restrain it through the relationship between Neo and Trinity.

Northcott, Michael. *An Angel Directs the Storm: Apocalyptic Religion and American Empire.* London: I. B. Tauris, 2004.

This study is one of a considerable number that have read the foreign policy of the George W. Bush administration in terms of an apocalyptic politics. In his inaugural address in 2001, President Bush revealed his faith in the nation's place in the apocalyptic struggle between the forces of good and evil. According to Northcott, these claims involved considerably more than simply "playing politics" in order to appeal to the voters from the so-called Christian Right. Rather, they announced something at the core of the way Bush and several of his advisors understood the geopolitical demands of the gospel in the modern world. The book locates this apocalypticism within considerably older, deeply rooted images of America as a chosen nation, a nation with a mission to civilize and police the world as "the liberator of humanity" (p. 3), the new world that brings redemptive light to the nations of the old. This stretches back to the Puritans, for whom the colony of New England was likened to the Promised Land, gifted to them by God, and the people as the new Israel. Accordingly, the colony was to become the site for the construction of the holy commonwealth. Northcott argues that this was the source for "American exceptionalism" and even eventually for the sense of "Manifest Destiny." Working from several speeches of Bush in the early 2000s, Northcott examines the idea that "America is in an apocalyptic struggle between the forces of good—America and those who ally themselves with her—and her enemies" (p. 7). This sensibility has been discernible in the hallowing of the nation's wars, especially those involving foreign conquest. The invasions of Afghanistan and Iraq occurred for reasons considerably deeper than that of self-defense after 9/11. They resulted from a "desire to reconfigure the Middle East to make it safe for what America regards as the only functioning democracy in the region, the nation of Israel" (p. 11). And this in itself is a consequence of the apocalyptic role of Israel among Christian Zionists. Moreover, the conflict was driven from the American side by "faith in unbridled capitalism" (p. 12). At certain points the book appears to alternate between apocalypticism and millenarianism, but these are not straightforwardly synonymous terms, even though in the nationalist imagination and its political agenda it is arguable that there is something of a confusion of themes, motifs, and narratives. The book, however, is aware that the contemporary political apocalypticism is a version of *pre*-millennialism or dispensationalism, a sensibility that began to appear more and more frequently in the nation's post-bellum history. This is a matter of urgency not so much for politics as for the church: "That Christian ethics can be put to such use is perhaps the greatest indictment of Christianity for many secular humanists in the first decade of the third millennium" (p. 13). Northcott hopes to repair the damage of what he identifies as a disordered version of Christianity: "American liberalism has colluded with apocalyptic religion in the construction of an imperial ideology of liberty because it has confined Christian thought and practice to the non-political, to the 'private', the 'personal' and to 'religious experience' or piety" (p. 110). For Northcott, "the key to reforming the apocalyptic subversion of true Christianity in America is the recovery of the truly anti-imperial message of the Bible, and of its founder, Jesus Christ" (p. 112). The kingdom of God is interpreted as the reign of God, but that does not indicate a future apocalyptic cataclysm. Rather, it has already come in Jesus Christ, challenging the law of domination and death in Jesus's nonviolent reordering of life and its relations away from imperial terror, its sacral justification, and its warrior ethos. Following Christ, the church is to be a counter-culture to the sacrificial demands of the imperial state, the latter being built on a mound of bodies. "A Christian account of the good can never identify any particular political structure or strategy, let alone a national strategy of pre-emptive warfare, as unambiguously good" (p. 141).

Pannenberg, Wolfhart. *Theology and the Kingdom of God*, trans. Richard John Neuhaus. Philadelphia: Westminster, 1969.

Pannenberg observes that his starting point is the kingdom of God as understood in terms of the eschatological future brought about by divine agency, in light of which human being and history are to be understood. He presents the future in terms of the coming of God, particularly as that future has appeared in Jesus Christ. In fact, his very ontology has a futural character, and so he advocates "an ontological priority of the future" (p. 139). This affects one's understanding of God's mode of being as the coming of God's rule. Pannenberg is careful, however, not to defer hope's action into the future, thereby leaving human hopers passive in the face of the coming of God. "God's rule is not simply in the future, leaving men to do nothing but wait quietly for its arrival" (p. 53). Jesus underscored the present impact of the imminent future of God's coming rule, even while "futurity is fundamental for Jesus' message" (p. 54). Here Pannenberg appeals to the categories of "anticipation" and "appearance." Properly grounded human hopes inspire action through the horizon of the kingdom of God, which therefore already determines and transforms "the present by creative love," even if that which "appears cannot be thought of as totally exhausted in the act of appearing" (pp. 81, 131). Certainly, "the future *wills* to become present; it tends towards its arrival in a permanent present" (p. 143). In lengthy reflections on the church as eschatological community, his refusal to privatize and individualize Christian hope, Pannenberg speaks of the church in terms of being "an anticipation of the new mankind, a mankind under the rule of God and his Spirit" (p. 74). Nonetheless, this does not give the church some special ecclesiastical light and authority, a possession to have and to hold that would permit a feeling of superiority over the world. "No, the Church is true to its vocation only as it anticipates and represents the destiny of all mankind, the goal of history." Only in fulfilling this vocation will the kingdom of God "manifest itself in and through the Church" (p. 77).

Pannenberg, Wolfhart. "The Task of Christian Eschatology." In *The Last Things: Biblical and Theological Perspectives on Eschatology*, ed. Carl E. Braaten and Robert W. Jenson, 1–13. Grand Rapids: Eerdmans, 2002.

Pannenberg admits that Christian doctrine has to engage in a critical conflict "with the mentality of our increasingly secular culture" (p. 1). Tackling Christian eschatological hope, he addresses secular concerns with that hope, and he refuses to provide an escapist option for hope as has "been effective in certain forms of Christian spirituality." Authentic Christian hope concretely "empowers the believer to affirm this present life, notwithstanding its fragility, affirm it in the light of a future consummation and transfiguration the achievement of which is beyond all human effort and potential" (p. 2). It is "the consummation and transfiguration of this our life on earth" (p. 7). This kind of hope cannot be reduced "to something additional to faith in God," an end-time supplement. Working from the image of the Synoptic Gospels' proclamation of the coming of the kingdom of God, Pannenberg recognizes the social effect of Christian hope that is bound up necessarily with "a hope for all humankind in communion with God" (p. 4). Such a comprehensive version of hope involves its consummation in the ultimate completion of human, and in fact all creaturely, existence brought about by God and destined from humanity's having been created by God in perfect peace and genuine justice.

Rahner, Karl. "Christology within an Evolutionary View of the World." In his *Foundations of Christian Faith: An Introduction to the Idea of Christianity,* trans. William V. Dych, 178–203. New York: Crossroad, 1978.

In this difficult text, Karl Rahner, arguably the most important Roman Catholic theologian of the twentieth century, attempts to identify what it is about human beings that enables them to hear the message of God in Christ, the God-Man. This he calls the "transcendental possibility in man" (p. 178). The mode of argument is what is called transcendental argument, or one that asks questions about the conditions for the way things are. The specific setting for the way Rahner asks his questions in this text is the evolutionary view of the world, which provides the "horizons of understanding" of the Christian's age and contemporaneity. Speaking in terms of transcendental possibilities, Rahner depicts humanity as being in essence "self-transcendence into God by means of God's Self-communication, a self-transcendence gratuitously made possible for him by God" (p. 179). This possibility is the divinely creative possibility that occurs definitively in and through the one who truly and fully self-transcends into God—Jesus Christ, the God-Man. Accordingly, "the Incarnation appears as the necessary and permanent beginning of the divinization of the world as a whole." This realization of the absolute fullness of being, Rahner admits, "has indeed already begun but is not yet complete." It involves "an active transformation of the material world itself" (p. 187). When Rahner speaks of "evolution," that movement of the world toward its divinization in God in Christ, or a fulfilling transcending of human spirit, he is speaking *theologically.* In other words, he is speaking about the eschatologically creative purposes of God, and what the world is within those purposes. The world is created to receive God's graciousness; human beings are those creatures engraced by God; that engracedness entails that human beings are only human when in relation beyond their selves (this he calls self-transcendence); this self-transcending or relational humanity is what Jesus Christ is, and in that sense he is the fulfillment of the world; we are human only insofar as we are becoming those who are in the process of self-transcendence or becoming self-conscious (those conscious of being who they are only as human in Christ); and hence the incarnation is natural to the world, and something for which the world was destined.

Rahner, Karl. "The Hermeneutics of Eschatological Assertions." In his *Theological Investigations,* volume 4, trans. Kevin Smyth, 323–46. Baltimore: Helicon, 1966.

This paper from 1954 addresses the issue of how to interpret eschatological statements. All such assertions are guided by certain hermeneutical principles or ways of understanding. Rahner argues that it is problematic to impose contemporary views and perspectives on texts that operate with different

principles, and so instead "we should ask what are the principles of hermeneutics suggested by Scripture itself, where it makes eschatological assertions"
(p. 325). Rahner rejects two broad approaches. The first is one that reduces
eschatological statements to statements about the faith and existence of the
Christian, as is evident in the "existentialist" approach of Rudolf Bultmann.
The second is one that understands eschatological statements to be blueprints
of coming history or forms of futurist soothsaying, as in the "apocalyptic"
approach. So Rahner rejects any ability to claim either that there is a certain and actual damnation of other people or that all will be saved. Instead,
Christian eschatology has only one theme: "the victory of grace in redemption
consummated," though this theme is "couched indeed in terms which safe-
guard God's mystery with regard to individual men as pilgrims and do not
say whether the individual is included in this certain triumph of grace—or
'left out'" (p. 340). In contrast to the two approaches rejected by Rahner, eschatological statements are directed toward the future rather than simply the
present (contra the existentialist approach), but have to do with the coming of
the mysterious God and are therefore not God-revealed predictions of future
events (contra the apocalyptic approach). Rahner focuses attention on the
experience of salvation and the events of the history of salvation "as it tends
to the future fulfilment which is and must be essentially hidden" (p. 342). This
leads him to claim that Jesus "Christ himself is the hermeneutical principle
of all eschatological claims" (pp. 342–43). Accordingly, "anything that cannot
be read and understood as a Christological assertion is not a genuine eschatological assertion" (p. 342).

Ratzinger, Joseph. *Eschatology: Death and Eternal Life*, trans. Michael Waldstein. Washington, DC: Catholic University of America Press, 1998.

Joseph Ratzinger's *Eschatology* is a clear and concise exposition of the last things,
focusing upon the church's belief in eternal life. He traces this belief through
the Scriptures, philosophical sources, and the tradition, drawing attention to
the embodied hope of resurrection. Contextually, it is instructive to note that
in his foreword he states: "My experience with this subject has been somewhat
curious. I began rather boldly with a set of theses which were then still uncom-
mon but are now almost universally accepted in Catholic circles: that is, I tried
to construct a 'de-Platonized' eschatology. However, the more I dealt with the
questions and immersed myself in the sources, the more the antitheses I had
set up fell to pieces in my hands and in their place I saw the inner logic of the
Church's tradition stand forth" (p. 11). The "Harnoration thesis," which is still held
sway over many of Ratzinger's early contemporaries, is the idea that Christianity
was obscured by its use of Greek philosophical sources, and consequently that
beliefs such as the distinction between soul and body, or Greek ideas of the
afterlife, became embedded within Christian doctrine. Rahner's text is both a

great resource and gateway into primary sources and a landmark in the modern history of the study of eschatology.

Ratzinger, Joseph. *Instruction on Certain Aspects of the "Theology of Liberation,"* http://www.vatican.va/roman_curia/congregations/cfaith/documents /rc_con_cfaith_doc_19840806_theology-liberation_en.html (accessed January 18, 2017).

Liberation theologies in Latin America were met with resistance from many within the ecclesial hierarchy. Famously, in a 1984 document Cardinal Joseph Ratzinger (later Pope Benedict XVI) criticized liberation theologians for their adoption of Marxist conceptuality. Ratzinger was unequivocally opposed to oppressive forces in Latin America such as "the seizure of the vast majority of the wealth by an oligarchy of owners bereft of social consciousness, the practical absence or the shortcomings of a rule of law, military dictators making a mockery of elementary human rights." Yet he remained categorically opposed to the use of Marxist conceptuality to oppose these forces: "The recognition of injustice is accompanied by a pathos which borrows its language from Marxism, wrongly presented as though it were scientific language." It is important to remember here that Ratzinger is a German intellectual, and Pope John Paul II, the pope at the time, was Polish. Both nations were directly affected by the growth in prominence of the USSR after World War II. The European experience of Marxism was rather different from the Latin American experience, and so there remained immense potential for misunderstanding. Ratzinger was worried that a Marxist notion of revolution and world history would overtake the centerpiece of Christian theology, Jesus Christ. In retrospect, one might read his and the liberation theologians' concerns as more sympathetic to one another than perhaps they realized at the time.

Robinson, J. A. T. *In the End, God.* London: James Clarke, 1950.

Robinson's book presents universal salvation, or the *apokatastasis*, as arising out of the sense of the omnipotence of the divine love revealed in Jesus Christ. In the New Testament there are two quite distinctive portrayals of the end, neither of which, in Robinson's view, is to be understood as dominating the other or as giving literal predictions: those texts that speak of a universal restoration of all things (e.g., 1 Cor. 15:24–28), and those texts that insist on a judgment that separates the saved and the lost (e.g., Matt. 25:31–46). From the latter "there is no ground whatever in the Bible for supposing that all men, simply because they are men, are 'going the same way'—except to Hell" (p. 108). However, "the sole basis for such a doctrine, as more than wishful thinking, is the work of God in Christ." From this gospel, he argues, we are directed to the one decisive act of God that has been given to, and accomplished for, the salvation of all.

This act will entail that God is ultimately all in all. It is from the doctrine of God—more precisely, from the omnipotence of divine love—that Robinson begins his argument toward maintaining that the biblical statements about the universal range of God's saving work are indeed eschatological claims, or claims about the future. It is inconceivable that this omnipotent love could fail to achieve its purposes, and the final loss of even one of God's creatures would constitute just such a failure. If any human being had the power to resist God's love forever, "this power would have shown itself to be stronger than God and thereby have reared a final disproof of the omnipotence of his love." In that case, "God would simply cease to be God" (p. 118). What about human freedom and the possibility of eschatological resistance to God's will? Robinson develops a compatibilist scheme in which human freedom has to be understood as being compatible with the victory of omnipotent love. It is precisely in submission to Christ, which takes place in unconditional response to the prompting of the Spirit, that true freedom is to be found. He confidently asserts that ultimately all will be saved because all, in time, will come to choose the salvation offered through Christ's atoning death and resurrection. In the end, "in a universe of love there can be no heaven which tolerates a chamber of horrors, no hell for any which does not at the same time make it hell for God" (p. 133).

Schillebeeckx, Edward. *God the Future of Man*, trans. N. D. Smith, chapter 6. London: Sheed and Ward, 1969.

While there are many interesting things about this eschatologically focused chapter, we will highlight just a few. Writing at a time of political ferment, Schillebeeckx endeavors to indicate the impact "eschatological hope" has to have on life in the world, if it is to be appropriate to its own content. He also observes not only the positive content of Christian hope but also its critical value, so that it is "a call to transcend what *we* have made—war, injustice, the absence of peace, the absence of love" (p. 184). These are all things "which would diminish man's being" (p. 197). This means that, in and through faith in the God of promise through Christ and in the Spirit, the Christian is engaged in opposing in hope all that resists God's salvation of the world, while recognizing that all human achievements are only partial and relative—in other words, they cannot be absolutized, finalized, and se-cured as if they were perfect expressions of the coming of God's salvation. While Schillebeeckx appreciates the way Freud and Marx have unmasked the childlike need for consolation that many seek in religion, he does regard Christian hope as more hopeful than Marxism, since he regards the latter as foreclosing possibilities for the future prematurely. Therefore, he argues, "without the dynamism of Christian hope straining towards an absolute future we are left with an ideological design of man which limits what is 'humanly desirable' in advance" (p. 197). Christian hope, then, strains toward a most radical commitment to the well-being of one's fellows, and that means toward "the humanization of the world, but directed towards the *eschaton*" (p. 199).

Schmemann, Alexander. *O Death, Where Is Thy Sting?*, trans. Alexis Vinogradov. Crestwood, NY: St. Vladimir's Seminary Press, 2003.

This short and highly readable book is the product of the transcription of a series of radio talks given by the Russian theologian on eschatological matters. In these presentations Schmemann broadly has two main concerns. The first has to do with efforts "to affirm the existence of another world" that unwittingly end up undermining "the reality and the value of this visible world" (p. 17). All of civilization, he claims, is permeated by a "passionate obsession to stifle this fear of death and sense of the meaninglessness of life" (p. 23), what Schmemann memorably terms turning the world into "a cosmic cemetery" (p. 82), or the sense of death as welcome release from the oppressiveness of the body. He argues that these efforts are unsatisfactory, since we simply have no knowledge of another world, and he connects his concern with the doctrine of creation, so that he is able to rhetorically ask, "can it really be that God created the world and life and all of its beauty, all of its possibilities, only in order that man would reject them and forgo all these glorious possibilities in the name of some unknown and only vaguely promised *other* world?" (p. 18). One must be careful to see what Schmemann is and is not doing here. He is not moving toward providing a glib account that all things are and will be well in any straightforward sense. In fact, his second determinative concern is with the way in which people console themselves in problematic ways over the matter of death. In contrast, Schmemann asks that the issues be approached without false and problem-evading hope. Accordingly, it is a powerful witness to observe that Jesus himself wept beside the grave of Lazarus without offering any glibly comforting message about the continuation of his friend's life in some otherworldly state, "a dream of another world" (p. 36). What the Christian witness provides is a witness to "a faith built on the annihilation of death and on the resurrection" (p. 20). This means that it is integral to the Christian proclamation to recognize that Jesus simply did not speak of the immortality of the soul, but rather promised the resurrection of the dead. This, among other things, entails that Christian hope cannot be a dematerializing or individualizing one. After all, "my body is my relationship to the world, to others; it is my life as communion and as mutual relationship" (p. 42). In this regard, the Christian confession of resurrection both speaks positively of the restoration of all things in the sacramental presence of the gracious God and resists "cheap and egotistical religion" (p. 51).

Tanner, Kathryn. "Eschatology without a Future?" In *The End of the World and the Ends of God: Science and Theology on Eschatology*, ed. John Polkinghorne and Michael Welker, 222–37. Harrisburg, PA: Trinity Press International, 2000.

Tanner's paper frames its reflections with concerns over end-time scenarios that have become increasingly common among scientists. "If the scientists are right, the world for which Christians hold out hope ultimately has no future" (p. 222). One theological strategy might be to delineate God's intervention in order to repair any possible damage and cosmic catastrophe. Tanner, however, refuses to take such a "God of the gaps" approach to the matter. Just as the doctrine of creation is not about cosmological beginnings, so eschatology is not about cosmological endings. Rather, it has to do with life lived in God's ongoing purposes, which embrace past, present, and future, in contrast to death as the separation of oneself from the source of life. "A Christian eschatology would have no more stake in whether or how the world ends than a Christian account of creation has in whether or how the world had a beginning (say, by means of a big bang)" (p. 224). Comprehensively cosmic, eschatology does not leave the world behind in a way that spiritualizes belief and reduces it "to a psychological, purely human, and private matter" (p. 224). Tanner opposes images of postmortem existence as an immortal state characterized by something like the existence we had before, only now no longer susceptible to death. Instead, she declares that mortal creatures are taken up into the life of God in the very life they have, in sheer gift, as those whose new identities are given in the purposeful work of the immortal God. Tanner addresses the issue of whether her approach weakens motivation for bringing about a better future for human beings and their world. Here she argues that being alive in the gift of God involves the task of living out the life of a holy people out of gratitude for God's giving. The life we are to live, then, empowers the struggle to overcome a death-dealing world that generates and sustains the impoverishment of existence through the inflicting of unjust suffering, community-ending exclusion, and hopelessness.

Teilhard de Chardin, Pierre. *The Divine Milieu: An Essay on the Interior Life.* New York: Harper & Row, 1960.

Pierre Teilhard de Chardin (1881–1955) was a French paleontologist, geologist, and priest of the Jesuit order. This companion to *The Phenomenon of Man* (see below) offers a vision of all things being bound up together, reunited in Christ. The descent of Christ our animates the world and unites human beings through love (p. 123). Accordingly, "the human layer of the earth is wholly and continuously under the organising influx of the incarnate Christ" (p. 124). Teilhard attempts to make sense of the image of the kingdom of God, and while he does have a pronounced sense of the eschatological unity of all things in

Christ, he interiorizes the concept of the kingdom of God itself. "The kingdom of God is within us" (p. 128). This process is the christification, the drawing of creation into its fulfillment in Christ, the time when "the presence of Christ . . . will suddenly be revealed—like a flash of light from pole to pole." The fulfillment (what Teilhard tends to refer to as the Pleroma, taken from the Greek word for fullness or perfection) occurs when all things are finally received and end in Christ, and this is named "christogenesis." This is not itself a natural product of the evolutionary process but is joined with the anthropogenesis, humanity becoming human, in salvation-history. The eschatological image is one of a hoped-for harmonious unification—"divinisation" (p. 154). This hope directs Christian action: "We must try everything for Christ; we must hope everything for Christ" (p. 154).

Teilhard de Chardin, Pierre. *The Phenomenon of Man*, trans. Bernard Wall. New York: Harper & Row, 1961.

Eschatology is bound up with Teilhard's account of creation and Christology, and it works out as the teleological or orthogenetic (a directional evolutionism) unfolding of a cosmic evolutionary scheme in which all things are drawn into the cosmically fulfilling eschatological life of God in Christ (Col. 1:15-17). In his work, evolution is the setting for considering salvation history. Teilhard surrounds this evolutionary account with metaphysical concepts, speaking of the movement of the evolutionary unfolding of the world from its alpha of the cosmosphere and biosphere through to the Omega Point (Rev. 1:8) that pulls all things toward itself. Evolution is a process of increasing complexity, and this complexity is what leads from the cosmosphere of particles through the biosphere of animal life-forms to the noosphere (Greek, "mind") or consciousness, the new age of the human world. This process Teilhard calls hominization, describing it as "an irreversibly 'personalising' universe," the evolution of human beings from the animal world to the consciousness of the noosphere (p. 290). In a striking phrase taken from evolutionary biologist Julian Huxley, Teilhard claims that human beings are creation becoming conscious of itself (p. 165). The fulfillment is "the end of the world: the overthrow of equilibrium, detaching the mind, fulfilled at last, from its material matrix, so that it will henceforth rest with all its weight on God-Omega. The end of the world: critical point simultaneously of emergence and emersion, of maturation and escape" (pp. 287-88).

Volf, Miroslav. *Exclusion and Embrace: A Theological Exploration of Identity, Otherness, and Reconciliation*, chapter 7. Nashville: Abingdon, 1996.

In this well-presented chapter, Volf turns particularly to the book of Revelation in order to address matters of violence and peace. The contrast that drives the chapter is that between the politics of Caesar and the political implications of

Christ's message of the kingdom of God: "In Pilate's world, truth and justice were the *fruits* of Caesar's sword. In Jesus' kingdom, truth and justice were *alternatives* to Caesar's sword" (p. 275). The problem Volf identifies is the way the church reaches, not for the crucified Christ, but for the resurrected and glorified Christ, in a premature triumphalism that ends up not rooting out violence but rather fostering it. Volf critically discusses Enlightenment projects for overcoming violence, concluding, along with Zygmunt Bauman, that destructive projects like the Holocaust were actually expressions of modernity. "If peace is what we are after, then a critique of the religious legitimation of violence—the critique of bellicose gods—is more urgent than reconciliation between religions" (p. 285). This provides a launchpad for Volf to critique religious attempts to justify violence and war: "without the principled assertion that it *is never appropriate to use religion to give moral sanction to the use of violence*, religious images and religious leaders will continue to be exploited by politicians and generals engaged in violence" (p. 286). So he rhetorically enjoins: "show me one warring party that does not think its war is just!" (p. 306). How is one to break this cycle of violence and its legitimating theology, especially in regard to matters of retaliation and retributive punishment? Volf discovers in the images of "the crucified Messiah (the theology of the cross) and the Rider on the white horse (the theology of judgment)" a refusal to "underwrite violence" and the "offer [of] important resources for living peacefully in a violent world" (p. 278). Among other things, these images can enable the rooting out, or unmasking, of the causes of violence and the rhetoric that is adopted to deceive as to the nature of those causes. More positively, these images also display the divine politics of transformatively setting aright the world of injustice and deception.

Webster, John. "Reading Scripture Eschatologically (I)." In *Reading Texts, Seeking Wisdom: Scripture and Theology*, ed. David F. Ford and Graham Stanton, 245–56. Grand Rapids: Eerdmans, 2003.

Webster's essay seeks to provide a theological account of the human activity of reading the Scriptures "as an instance of how reconciled sinners, sanctified by the Spirit, are engaged by God's communicative presence" (p. 245). That means that the activity of reading the Scriptures is caught up in God's making of the new reality in Christ, realized by the Spirit. That activity of reading well entails that "we have to be made into certain kinds of readers" (p. 249).

Whitehead, Alfred North, *Process and Reality*, corrected edition, ed. David Ray Griffin and Donald W. Sherburne. New York: Free Press, 1978.

"Process theology" is a blanket term used for theologies that derive much of their philosophical content and language from the thought of Alfred North Whitehead (1861–1947). What distinguishes Whitehead's process philosophy is its preoccupation with undoing or significantly reframing what it considers to be metaphysically problematic assumptions on the part of classical theology and metaphysics. These include notions about God such as God being simple (not being a composite substance), omnipotent (all-powerful), omniscient (all-knowing), immutable (unchangeable), and impassible (unable to suffer). Whitehead's thought has philosophical predecessors in modern philosophical theology, particularly in the thought of Henri Bergson, G. W. F. Hegel, Baruch Spinoza, and Gottfried Leibniz. Whitehead developed a distinct vocabulary for speaking of God's relationship to time. He sought to understand how people change and grow through time. Each moment of human experience is described as already passing. Time moves too fast for us to grasp it, as it does not stop. But we can reflect on our past at a distance, and in doing that we experience it again. God, for Whitehead, experiences all things and folds all things into God's self. God "emerges" with the world. Everything that has happened is therefore in some sense available for God to remember. This allows Whitehead to talk about God as experiencing time with creation. God does not foresee the end; God arrives at the end only when we do. It also allows Whitehead to talk about the immortality of creation, because God includes all things in God's own experience imperishably. Further, because God has this experience built up, God is also able to see all the possible futures that might emerge. God, acting with the creature, sees these possibilities open and close as human and divine freedom weave in and out of one another. This is not random, however. Whitehead thinks that Christianity betrayed its most basic instincts as it capitulated to the Roman Empire. But God persists as the one allowing us the freedom to act. God remains one who does not grasp after power. Whitehead states, "The notion of God as the 'unmoved mover' is derived from Aristotle. . . . The notion of God as 'eminently real' is a favourite doctrine of Christian theology. The combination of the two in the doctrine of an aboriginal, eminently real, transcendent creator, at whose fiat the world came into being, and whose imposed will it obeys, is the fallacy which has infused tragedy into the histories of Christianity and Mahometanism [Islam]. When the Western world accepted Christianity Caesar conquered; and the received text of Western theology was edited by his lawyers. . . . The brief Galilean vision of humility flickered throughout the ages, uncertainly. . . . The Church gave unto God the attributes which belonged exclusively to Caesar" (p. 347). Whitehead's God has a politics, and this politics is a vision of the good that never fully arrives because God is vulnerable to the freedom of the creature. Reality is continually emerging and changing. Hope, then, is rethought, not in terms of a fixed end, but as a process of becoming.

Wright, Tom. *The Myth of the Millennium*. London: Azure, 1999.

This is a small book written for a general, nonspecialist readership. Writing at the turn of the millennium, with the hopes and fears that that time generated, Wright rejects a number of popular claims that were made about the millennium in order "to free people from the tyranny of a literal understanding of 'apocalyptic'" and millennium (p. 27). He does this in order to repair current ways of living and planning for the future. The year 2000 is "just another accident of our accounting system," he argues, and any greater (apocalyptic) significance should not be read into it. Augustine and others read Revelation 20 not literally but symbolically. Opposing the dualism that often features in apocalyptic accounts, Wright argues that in the epistles of the apostle Paul "there is a strong incentive to work, in the present, to anticipate the new world in every possible way. Those who are grasped by the vision of God's new world unveiled in Jesus's resurrection are already sharing in that newness, and are called to produce, in the present time, more and more signposts to point to this eventual and glorious future" (p. 41). These are deeds that embody hope, justice, mercy, and freedom for the well-being of one's neighbor.

Wright, Tom. *Surprised by Hope.* London: SPCK, 2007.

For what may we hope? Wright suggests that "most people simply don't know what orthodox Christian belief might be" (p. 19). Generally, Christian hope is regularly assumed to refer to the belief in an afterlife. However, there are different ways of expressing this, and these assume different beliefs about God, the world, and the good life. Taking his cues primarily from the Scriptures, but in conversation with some literature and particularly a series of relevant Christian hymns, Wright critiques the devaluation of present reality as if Christians are to "go to heaven." He maintains that "there is very little in the Bible about 'going to heaven when you die', and not a lot about post-mortem hell either" (p. 25). Critiquing the myth of evolutionary optimism, the transit of the immortal soul, and the Christian version of a happily-ever-after approach to hope, his positive proposal may be summed up as follows: "to live as resurrection people in between Easter and the final day, with our Christian life, corporate and individual, in both worship and mission, as a sign of the first and a foretaste of the second" (p. 41). Accordingly, hope is what emerges and takes shape "when you suddenly realize that a different worldview is possible, a worldview in which the rich, the powerful and the unscrupulous do not after all have the last word" (p. 87).

Index

Agamben, Giorgio, 27
Antichrist, the, 9–10, 12, 71, 72, 95
apocalypticism, 1–27; biblical, 2–5; medieval, 6–10
apokatastasis (universal salvation), 40, 76, 103, 109
apophaticism, 35–36
Armageddon, 4, 21
Athanasius, 96–100, 106
Augustine, 6, 60–61, 63–68

Bale, John, 69
Balthasar, Hans Urs von, 29, 30, 36–40, 50, 109
Barth, Karl, 26–27, 100–104, 109
Bible, the, 16, 22, 84–89; apocalyptic, 2–5, 80; eschatological images, xi, 83; interpretation, xi–xii, 4–5, 90–91; myth and demythologization, 40–43; political, 52–63
Bloch, Ernst, 74–75
Boff, Clodovis, 79, 81–82
Boff, Leonardo, 79–82
Bonhoeffer, Dietrich, 40
Brightman, Thomas, 72
Bulkeley, Peter, 72
Bultmann, Rudolf, 28, 37, 40–45, 106
Butler, Judith, 46

Calvin, John, 11

Charles I, 70–72
Charles II, 71
Coakley, Sarah, 46, 49–50
Cocceus, Johannes, 18
Colovius, Abraham, 51
Constantine I, 61–63
Coppola, Francis Ford, 1
Cotton, John, 72
Cromwell, Thomas, 69
cross, theology of the, 12

Daniélou, Jean, 30
Darby, John Nelson, 19
deification, 94, 99
Descartes, René, 106
destiny, manifest, 73–74
dispensationalism, 5, 18–21
Duche, Jacob, 73

Eck, Johannes, 11
Edward VI, 70
Elizabeth I, 69–70, 72
eternal life, xi, 13, 67, 87–89, 103
Eusebius of Caesarea, 62

feminism, 45–50
Foxe, John, 69

Gregory VII, 6–7
Gutiérrez, Gustavo, 74, 78–82

149

Index

Twisse, William, 71

Washington, George, 73
Weiss, Johannes, 22–24, 42
Winthrop, John, 72
Wollstonecraft, Mary, 45

Wrede, William, 24

Yoder, John Howard, 27

Žižek, Slavoj, 5, 27